How to Analyze People 101

Speed-reading Other People through
Simple Behavior. Quick Ways You Can
Read Others Using Body Language
Training, Personality Types, and the
Principles of Human Psychology

Written By

Brandon D. Evans

this book.

By reading this document, the reader agrees that under no circumstances is the author responsible for any losses, direct or indirect, which are incurred as a result of the use of information contained within this document, including, but not limited to, — errors, omissions, or inaccuracies.

Table of Contents

Introduction

Language has to do with communication. We tend to believe language refers to just spoken words. However, you may be shocked to find out that more than eighty percent of what we communicate with one another is unspoken. This communication comes in the form of nonverbal signs that we send to one another via facial expressions, eye contact, postures, gestures, and a host of sounds.

This communication is body language. We utilize it every time we communicate, with some signs being more natural than others, and the majority of the time we are not even aware we are using it. We begin to learn body language in childhood, similar to how we learn to communicate in our native tongue by picking up words and what they mean from our parents and others around. However, the core difference is that even though we can correct errors in our spoken language, it is easy to misinterpret or miss them in body language. So, it is possible for you to live your life without realizing you are not communicating properly.

This area is where this book can help. These cues and signals pass information regarding our intentions, motives, and feelings. We use body language to pass all forms of messages and interpretations that a lot of us do not appreciate.

You only have to imagine the individuals you dislike or admire the most to understand how important body language is. The ones oozing charisma who people seem to be drawn to, the ones who just seem to annoy you, the quiet ones—something about their presence conveys a message to you.

Because we don't understand the link between body language and the mind, we often do not make the best of our relationships with others or ourselves. It is only when we take a closer look that we begin to divulge information about others and ourselves that we failed to see before.

If you believe that you are not putting in your best at work, in your personal relationships, or just in the way you interact with others, then this book could be relevant. You most likely want to learn how to become more apt in utilizing body language and understanding how other individuals use it.

Hopefully, when you finish this book, you will have an idea of the significance of body language and how it can aid in enhancing your relationships and the way you interact with others.

Chapter 1: How Does Body Language Relate to Human Psychology?

How Body Language Is Related to Human Psychology

Human psychology is the science of the mind and behavior. It includes the unconscious and conscious phenomena, alongside thoughts and feelings. As an academic discipline, it has a broad scope and a distinct interest that when considered as one, look to understand the brain's emergent properties and its range of manifestations.

For psychologists who want to fully understand human psychology, they focus on mental processes and behavior. These include intelligence, emotion, personality, perception, and brain functioning. This focus goes further into the interaction between individuals like family resilience and interpersonal relationships, etc.

Psychologists of varying orientations also put the unconscious mind into consideration.

What Is Body Language?

Body language is a form of nonverbal communication that depends on body motions like posture, gestures, and facial expressions to pass messages.

It is possible to use body language unconsciously and consciously. It may come with a verbal message or act as a speech substitute.

How do they both relate?

Body language is an essential part of human psychology. To completely understand the psychology of humans, one needs to read a lot of factors, and body language is one of them. Basically, without body language, you would be unable to grasp human psychology completely.

Body language offers information and more elaborate insights you would not have observed previously. It is a fertile field that must be explored if you want to understand the way humans think and behave.

What Does My Behavior Display?

Irrespective of whether you are networking or making a presentation or trying to detect a lie from someone, body language is usually the key in uncovering or creating the actual meaning of a message.

Before you made the first statement in your life, body language was already a relevant aspect of your life. Professor Albert Mehrabian, in his book *Silent Messages*, concludes that fifty-five percent of communication occurs via body language. Individuals instantaneously and intuitively develop a perception in the initial moments they set their eyes on you, and body language confirms, dispels, or builds those impressions.

With this fact in consideration, here are some ways body language can help in revealing emotions.

You Are Either Very Anxious or Lying

Terrible or nonexistent eye contact could be a symptom of nervousness, lying, or terror in Western cultures. Other signals consist of licking lips, shaking, sweating, and moving the hand to the face to cover the eyes or mouth.

Sadly, it is sometimes easy to confuse lying with a terrible case of butterflies, but it makes a lot of sense. When an individual lie, they typically are not confident in their message, and their body portrays that. When you are anxious, you do not have self-assurance, and it is obvious.

You Are Heading for the Top

Energy, charisma, open body language, eye contact. These are the indications of success and of an individual who understands how to communicate properly with their body. They can calmly sit down while still exuding energy or come up to you with a confident handshake. They are also able to align themselves with the room while they speak and are in total control of their gestures and movements.

Imagine an individual with crossed arms whose feet are firmly on the ground. You are trying to converse when his face starts to flush red, and he points a finger at you. This is the moment where you get ready to defend yourself or find a means to quickly dissolve the situation.

It Could Show You Are Bored

It is easy to observe boredom in an individual from afar. When individuals head into standby mode, they have the tendency to focus on crucial things like reading words on their pen or looking into space. Boredom is not easy to hide because it signifies a conflict between the physical presence of a person and his unconscious desires.

It Reveals Submission

The body language of a submissive individual show helplessness. The physical signs of an individual who is overly forgiving become apparent when an individual is nervous and wants to stay away from any form of conflict and criticism. Their faces have a sheepish look, and they stay relatively motionless to avert bringing attention to themselves. They may also leave their face pointed downward.

You Have My Attention

Interest establishes itself with nodding, good eye contact, and leaning toward the subject of interest. It does not involve continuously taking a sneak peek at your phone or glancing continually at your wristwatch.

Most times, we watch or listen passively, do not assimilate or process and secure the information. When you have the attention of a person, they display proactive body language.

How the Body Reveals Emotions

Have you ever thought about how the body reveals emotions? Well, you are not alone. Lots of people do. But the great news is that a group of biomedical engineers provided a solution to this old question.

They drew the way the body reacts to emotions in 700 people and observed that the patterns were similar irrespective of where the person lived.

The study, done by a team from Finland, depends on visual feedback offered by candidates from Taiwan, Sweden, and Finland. External Sensors or Brain Mapping could have been utilized in measuring the physiological outputs and neurological changes like body temperature and sweat. However, by offering the subjects two human body figures and requesting that they point out precisely where they felt activity decreasing or increasing, the team was able to amass intimate information that was normally not possible. It means the study depends on the self-assessment of candidates correctly without bias.

Although each emotion created an explicit map of bodily sensation, researchers did point out some regions of overlap. Basic emotions like fear and anger resulted in a rise in sensation in the upper area of the chest likely corresponding to increases in the rate of respiration and pulse. The only emotion that was tested that caused a rise in the sensation all around the body was happiness.

The findings improved the understanding of researchers on the way we process emotions. Despite differences in language and culture, it seems our physical experience regarding feelings is amazingly steady across various populations. The researchers feel that additional growth of these bodily sensation maps may lead to a new method of pointing out and treating emotional disorders in the future.

If you are interested in checking out the full study, you can find it here,

https://www.pnas.org/content/early/2013/12/26/13216641 11?with-ds=yes

How Body Language Reveals the Real You

Body language is a part of communication that is often overlooked. However, it is crucial in providing support for your spoken words and message. Although the majority of the time, it takes place automatically. You will be able to learn to keenly manage your gestures, postures, and facial expression. Once you learn your body language, you will undoubtedly get a more elaborate understanding of the individuals around you and significantly enhance the impact of your ability to persuade others.

The Connection to the Limbic System

What Is the Limbic System?

The limbic system is a complicated placement of structures

that lies on both parts of the thalamus, underneath the cerebrum. It consists of the hippocampus, hypothalamus, amygdala, and numerous other areas close by. It seems to be majorly responsible for our emotional life and has much to do with the creation of memories.

Parts of the Limbic System

Hypothalamus

The hypothalamus is a little area of the brain situated underneath the thalamus on both parts of the third ventricle. The ventricles are parts in the cerebrum filled with cerebrospinal fluid. They also link to the spine's fluid.

The hypothalamus lies above the pituitary gland and just within the two tracts of the optic nerves. The hypothalamus is one of the busiest aspects of the brain, and its main concern has to do with homeostasis.

Homeostasis has to do with taking something back to a set point. It functions like a thermostat. When surroundings become too cold, the thermostat passes the information to the furnace, which then comes on. When your room heats up, and the temperature surpasses a specific point, it sends another signal that informs the furnace to turn off.

The hypothalamus has the responsibility of regulating your

response to pain, thirst, hunger, sexual satisfaction, levels of pleasure, aggressive behavior, and anger among others. It also controls how the autonomic nervous system functions, which also means it helps in regulating elements like breathing, blood pressure, arousal, and pulse in response to emotional situations.

The hypothalamus gets input from a range of sources. The vagus nerve offers it information about the gut distention or how full your tummy is as well as information about your blood pressure.

In the reticular formation in the brainstem, it attains information regarding the temperature of the skin. From the optic nerve, it attains information relating to darkness and light. The unusual nerves lining the ventricles provides it with information about the cerebrospinal fluid's contents like toxins that result in vomiting.

From other areas of the limbic system alongside the olfactory nerves, it attains information that aids in regulating sexuality and eating. The hypothalamus also possesses some receptors that offer it information regarding blood temperature and ion balance.

In a recent discovery, it seems we have a protein known as leptin that is released by fat cells when we eat too much. The hypothalamus seemingly senses the leptin levels in the bloodstream and responds by reducing appetite. It also seems that there are individuals who possess a gene mutation that creates leptin and their bodies are unable to inform the hypothalamus that they have eaten enough. But a lot of individuals who are overweight do not possess this mutation, so it still requires much research.

The hypothalamus passes instruction to the remainder of the body in two methods. First is the autonomic nervous system. It lets the hypothalamus have complete control of things like sweating, breathing, blood pressure, and digestion alongside all the parasympathetic and sympathetic functions.

The other means by which the hypothalamus controls things is through the pituitary gland. It is chemically and neutrally linked to the pituitary, which then pushes hormones known as releasing factors to the bloodstream.

Hippocampus

The hippocampus is made up of two horns curving back from the amygdala. It seems to be very crucial in transforming present thoughts in your mind into thoughts you will not forget in the long run. If the hippocampus suffers damage, a person would be unable to create new memories and would instead live in a world where all they experience fades off while memories from before the damage remain untouched. Many individuals who experience this damage end up getting institutionalized.

Amygdala

The amygdala is two masses of neurons that are almond shaped on either part of the thalamus at the end of the hippocampus. When it is electrically stimulated, the response animals give is aggression. Also, when you take out the amygdala, animals no longer react to stimuli that would have previously caused a sexual response or fear. They also do not react to things that may have resulted in rage previously.

Other Related Areas

Besides these major areas, there are other parts in the structures close to the limbic system that are intimately linked to it.

- The **cingulate gyrus** is the potion of the cerebrum that is closest to the limbic system. It offers a route from the thalamus to the hippocampus. It seems to have the responsibility of focusing your attention on events that are emotionally relevant and for relating memories to pain and scent.

- The **ventral tegmental area** includes pathways for dopamine that are in charge of pleasure. Individuals who have suffered damage here tend to have issues attaining pleasure in life and often turn to drugs, gambling, alcohol, and sweets.

- The **basal ganglia** lie on the sides and over the limbic system. They are connected tightly to the cortex above them. They are accountable for reward experiences, focusing attention, and repetitive behaviors.

- The **prefrontal cortex** is the area of the frontal lobe lying ahead of the motor area. It is liked closely to the limbic system. Aside from being involved in making plans, thinking of the future, and taking steps, it is also involved in the exact dopamine routes as the ventral tegmental area. It equally plays a role in addiction and pleasure.

The Autonomic Nervous System

This area has a crucial role to play in our emotional life. It comprises of two parts that function contrary to one another. The sympathetic nervous system is the first one. It begins in the spinal cord and heads to a range of locations in the body. Its function is to ready the body for the forms of tedious activities that have to do with fight or flight.

When the sympathetic nervous system is triggered, it results in the following:

- Dilates the pupils

- Opens the eyelids

- Rouses the sweat glands

- Enhances the heart's rate

- Impedes the emissions in the digestive system

- Contracts the blood vessels in the remainder of the body

One of the most crucial effects is making the adrenal glands let out epinephrine into the bloodstream. Epinephrine is a potent hormone that makes numerous aspects of the body respond in a manner that is almost similar to the sympathetic nervous system. Because it is in the bloodstream, it requires slightly more time for the effects to stop. It is for this reason that it sometimes takes time before you can get calm again once you have gotten angry.

The sympathetic nervous system equally takes in data, mostly having to do with pain from the internal organs. Because the nerves that take information relating to organ pain travel along similar routes with those that carry information regarding pain from the body surface areas, the information sometimes gets mixed up. It is known as referred pain. A good example is the pain felt by some individuals on the arm and shoulder when having a heart attack.

The other aspect of the autonomic nervous system is known

as the **parasympathetic nervous system**. It is rooted in the lower back spinal cord and the brain stem. Its duty is to bring back the body from the emergency status it is put into by the sympathetic nervous system.

When there is parasympathetic arousal, a few of the effects are:

- Constricting of the pupils

- Activating of salivary glands

- Reducing heart rate

- Stimulating stomach and lung secretions

- Stimulating lung activities

The parasympathetic nervous system also possesses sensory capacities. It receives data relating to carbon dioxide levels in the blood and blood pressure among others.

The **enteric nervous system** is an aspect of the autonomic nervous system we don't talk about frequently. They are the nerves that aid in regulating stomach activity. When you feel butterflies in your stomach when you get anxious, this nervous system is responsible.

How Is Body Language Connected to the

Limbic System?

When something has to do with nonverbal behavior, the limbic part of the brain is responsible because it naturally responds to our surroundings and the stimulus it consists of. The behaviors our limbic brain produces are a more honest response over those regulated by the neocortex.

In essence, the limbic brain regulates emotional body language making it our top means of indicating what the body feels. The limbic brain is responsible for controlling the torso, hands, feet, and head when an individual is feeling ashamed or embarrassed, happy or excited, fearful or sad. The limbic system is wired into our nervous system and goes with us back in time through our evolution.

Although our neocortex can sometimes subdue the limbic brain, it is only possible when it is not preoccupied with other things. The neocortex has the responsibility of carrying out complicated conscious tasks like engineering and calculus, etc. So when it is turned off completely or overwhelmed, the body accidentally lets out emotional body language that others can read. The neocortex, because it is controlled consciously, is the least honest and least reliable aspect of the brain.

Research has shown that during deception, the neocortex is the most active region of the brain. This reason is why it has been termed the lying brain. Deceivers may have the ability to take charge of the words they utilize in describing their thoughts, but they are unable to control the way they react to these words. They are also unable to control the expressions that they let out. This inability is precisely how we can read stress and anger and also nab liars.

When thinking of the limbic system, try to consider the unplanned response that occurs when a loud bang startles us. Instinctively, our bodies become tense, our hand is drawn inward, and our heads hide in our torso while the nervous system places our heart in high speed via a burst of adrenaline.

It is the same area of the brain that makes your hands shake or feet fidget when you are excited. It is also the one that results in sweaty hands when dealing with pressure. Our limbic system also heads into hyperdrive when a person wins a lottery or when we see a loved one, we have not seen in a long time. Irrespective of what you do, you would not be able to prevent this reaction from occurring. The only possibility is to learn to reduce behaviors like clenching the hands together to minimize shaking when excited or inserting the legs behind a chair to keep them in place when you want to run off.

But by doing these actions, they reveal body language that tells others the neocortex is making efforts to subdue the instinctual brain, thus creating another leak of body language we can read. At an accident scene, it is fully expected that the limbic system takes over creating discomfort, nervousness, and shaking. Thus, if the cops get there, they will consider something wrong if the caller is completely relaxed and calm while the victim is almost dead and bloodied.

Naturally, the calm individual will be pulled aside as the prime witness. Therefore, we need to always watch out for limbic responses and link them to context so we are aware when something is wrong. When limbic responses cease, we are aware that the motivation for their production has also ceased, so we must then locate the reason.

The limbic brain is the aspect of our brain that is in charge of our root processes. To understand this concept, think about the activities of a lizard. Because it is cold-blooded, it looks for sun to hasten his metabolism, drinks when it is thirsty, eats when hungry, and either fights, freezes, or flees when scared. It does not do calculus or construct huge buildings because it does not have the ability, but irrespective of that, it stays alive because the limbic system informs it on all the necessary things to do.

In terms of evolution, our limbic system is the same. It informs us when to be scared and what we should do— minimize movement so our assailants can't find us, freeze, run and point our feet to the appropriate direction, or let our hearts start pumping so we can run. It is also in charge of our root emotions. It informs our feet to jump in excitement and move. It also tells the feet to fidget with readiness to leave when we are bored.

Basically, without the limbic system, there would be no body language to read in the first place.

Chapter 2: Body Language 101

Body Language and the Importance of Nonverbal Communication

Body language is a kind of nonverbal communication where individuals use physical behaviors instead of words in conveying or expressing information. These kinds of behaviors consist of body posture, facial expression, eye movement, gestures, and use of space as well as touch.

Here, we will be focusing on how to interpret human body language. It is also called kinesics.

Body language is not the same as sign languages. Sign languages are complete languages similar to spoken ones that come with their complicated grammar systems. They are also able to show the basic properties you can find in every language.

On the other hand, body language does not possess a grammar system. You need to broadly interpret it as opposed to having an obvious meaning that corresponds to a specific movement. So, it isn't a language similar to sign language, and it is only called a language as a result of popular norms.

What is Nonverbal Communication?

Nonverbal communication is the act of passing across a feeling, idea, or thought using facial expressions, posture, and physical gestures. According to a study carried out at UCLA, it was proven that most of communication is not verbal. Although the precise statistics of the study, which showed that just seven percent of any message was transmitted via words, fifty-five percent via nonverbal components like gestures and postures and thirty-eight percent via vocal components like tone are doubtful.

How Does Nonverbal Communication Work?

Nonverbal communication has a crucial role to play in our lives. It can enhance the capacity of an individual to engage, relate, and create relevant relations in everyday life. When individuals have better knowledge of this kind of communication, it may aid them in developing more powerful relationships with others. Frequently called body language, nonverbal communication can take a range of forms and can be interpreted in numerous ways by various individuals, mostly across cultures. Even an absence of these nonverbal cues can have a meaning and is a kind of nonverbal communication.

Every movement and blend of body movements like changes in posture, eye direction, limb gestures, and facial expressions gives a signal to other individuals. These cues could either be obvious or subtle and might be conflicting. An individual may say something while the body languages transmit a completely different message, something that is usually the case when the person is being deceptive. Because nonverbal communication is frequently natural, faking it is not easy, and it is a more accurate indication of how an individual feel.

Kinds of Nonverbal Communication

The kinds of nonverbal communication are numerous and varied. They can also offer broad perception into the feelings or thoughts of an individual. The kinds of nonverbal communication can be classified to better understand their place in daily interactions:

- **Posture**: the body's position on its own and the way it relates to others

- **Gesture**: the motion of the limbs or head

- **Eye Contact and Movements**: the focus and direction of an individual's eyes

- **Body Movements**: any movement of the body

- **Facial Expression**: any motion and changes of the facial structure

- **Voice Tone**: the variety of pitch in the voice that might communicate something aside from spoken words. For example, sarcasm may give the words of an individual an utterly distinct meaning.

Nonverbal communication is frequently used alongside verbal communication to support, repeat, contradict, and emphasize a verbal message. It is also utilized in replacing verbal messages.

Nonverbal Communication's Role in Relationships

The nonverbal cues of an individual may be less difficult to read by a family member, partner, or close friend. In close relationships, this profound understanding on a nonverbal level may encourage increased closeness or strengthen bonds. This understanding is the case when it corresponds with what is being said by one partner or friend in a relationship.

But when something feels wrong, it may not be as easy for individuals to keep things away from those they share a close relationship with, and efforts to do so may result in conflicts or miscommunications in the relationship. Since nonverbal communication is not often conscious, the way people interact nonverbally may reveal an underlying problem not readily obvious in the relationship.

Principles of Body Language Intelligence

The following are a few principles of body language intelligence:

Body Language Precedes Words

Individuals say and do things in response to what others say and do. These external happenings act as triggers or cues that inspire innate responses.

Cues could equally be internal. For example, where concerns and thoughts result in a change in the position of the body. You may also ask, "Considering their body language, what could they be feeling or thinking?"

Cues are a crucial aspect of conditioning where actions and emotions are paired with a cue such that when the cue shows up, it triggers a range of feelings and likely associated actions that the individual may try suppressing. This cue response could also be natural, like the way some creatures cause a fear response.

Context Is Everything

Context may impact how a person acts, feels, and thinks. What is happening in the immediate surroundings could have an obvious effect. For example, when men are around appealing young ladies, they will indulge more in posturing and preening.

The broader context of an individual's life may have an impact on their body language. It typically indicates excitement, anxieties, and anticipation. If you are not aware of such modifiers, it could have a severe effect on your efforts to read their body language.

Search for Clusters

While changes in body language can show up as single happenings, like the folding of arms, they often show up as a group of diverse movements that take place at the same time or one after the other. For example, an individual may cross their arms, change their posture, lean back slightly, frown, and purse their lips all as simultaneous evidence of disagreement.

Clusters of body movement send obvious signs when they all specify the same thing. This awareness may occur when each has a related meaning, or where the entire group of movement merges to create one definition.

At times, cluster movements oppose one another. For example, when an individual rubs his nose, which shows a possible deception, and smiles. The subsequently mixed signals will likely result in you feeling uncomfortable, and it would be smart to be vigilant for these kinds of gut feelings while searching for why you may be feeling this way.

Character

The general character of the other individual is a factor that can compound and explain a lot. An individual who is an extrovert, for example, may show regular and large body movements, while an individual who is more introverted may utilize more precise gestures.

Confusing these personality qualities for others like timidity is easy. In a bid to categorize others, we frequently misread limited body signs and then filter things we see using these inaccurate mental models.

Mood, temperament, and short-term emotions can also function as modifiers that have an impact on body language, making it much harder to interpret. If you can determine the present emotional state of a person, you will be able to apply this insight in your interpretation and attain a better understanding of the actual meanings of their motions.

Sudden Changes Are Relevant

A crucial thing to look out for are changes. For example, when an individual scratch their nose suddenly, it could be a sign of discomfort.

When you observe changes in body language, search for cues that may have caused the transition. For example, when an individual suspected of telling lies is asked a question and he looks away.

Individuals in sales are always on the lookout for body language changes like subtle cues, positive responses, and leaning forward as signs that a client is becoming persuaded. The salesperson then utilizes this knowledge as a sign to head to the next phase in closing the deal.

Rules for Accurately Reading People and Why Analyzing People Is Important

The capacity to read other individuals will have a great impact on your dealings with them. When you have an understanding of the feelings of another individual, you will be able to adapt your communication and message style to ensure it is attained in the best method possible.

But what are the things you should be watching out for that can aid you in reading someone accurately?

The First Strategy: Notice Body Language Cues

According to research, words account for just seven percent of how we converse, while our voice tone is thirty percent. The highest is the body language, which accounts for fifty-five percent.

Do not try too hard to read body language cues. Do not get too analytical or intense. Remain fluid and relaxed. Sit back, be comfortable, and observe.

Below are a few things to look out for:

- **Take Note of Appearance**

When you read others, observe the following: Are they putting on well-polished shoes and a power suit, dressed for triumph, signaling ambition?

T-shirt and jeans, signifying comfort and a casual look? A close-fitting top showing cleavage that indicates a seductive choice? A pendant like a Buddha or a cross indicating spiritual standards?

- **Observe Posture**

When reading the posture of others, ask yourself: Do they cower or walk indecisively, which is an indication of low self-esteem? Do they place their head high, a sign of confidence?

Does the individual swagger with their chest puffed out, which is an indication of a huge ego?

- **Look Out for Physical Motions**

Distance and leaning: Notice when individuals lean. Typically, individuals lean away from those they do not like and toward those they do.

Hiding hands: When individuals place their hands in their pockets, on their laps, or behind them, it indicates they are trying to hide something.

Crossed legs and arms: This position proposes anger, defensiveness, or self-protection. When individuals cross their legs, they tend to face the toes of the top leg in the direction of the individual with whom they are most comfortable.

- **Translate Facial Expression**

Emotions can be written on our faces. Deep frown lines indicate overthinking or worry. Smiling with crow's feet close to the eyes is an indication of joy. Teeth grinding and clenched jaw indicate tension. Pursed lips signify bitterness, anger, or contempt.

Gut feelings take place quickly; they are a natural reaction. They act as your truth meter and let you know if you should trust a person.

- **Sense the Goosebumps**

These are wonderful instinctive prickles that let us know we resonate with individuals who inspire or move us, or we are

36

having a conversation that hits the spot.

Goosebumps also occur when you experience déjà vu, which is a feeling that you used to know a person even though you have not met before.

- **Watch Out for Flickers of Insight**

When conversing with individuals, a bulb may light up about an individual, which comes in an instant. You must remain alert, or you may miss it. We tend to head to the subsequent thoughts so quickly that we lose these vital insights.

- **Look Out for Intuitive Compassion**

At times you will be able to feel the physical emotions and symptoms of individuals in your body, which is a powerful kind of compassion. So, while reading individuals, notice things like whether your arm hurts when it did not previously or if you are upset or sad after a meeting. To find out if this is empathy, you need to get feedback.

The Third Strategy: Perceive Emotional Energy

Emotions are spectacular expressions of our energy or the vibe we let out. We record these using intuition. It feels great to be around some individuals; they enhance your vitality and mood.

On the other hand, others drain you; you impulsively want to leave their vicinity. You can feel this subtle energy feet or inches from the body, even though it is not visible. It is known as "Chi" in Chinese medicine, a crucial vitality to health.

Tactics for Reading Emotional Energy

- ### Sense the Presence of Individuals

Presence is the total energy we let out. It is not essentially consistent with behavior or words. It is the emotional air that surrounds us like the sun or a rain cloud.

When you read individuals, observe whether they have a friendly presence that draws you in. Or are you getting the jitters, which make you back off?

- ### Pay Attention to the Eyes of Individuals

Our eyes convey commanding energies, similar to the way the brain possesses an electronic signal that extends past the body. Even without research, we intuitively know that the eyes send energy.

Take a moment to observe the eyes of individuals. Are they angry? Caring? Mean? Is the individual at home in their eyes, showing an aptitude for intimacy? Or do they seem to be hiding or shielded?

- **Notice How a Touch, Hug, and Handshake Feels**

We send emotional energy via physical contact similar to an electrical current. Ask yourself whether a hug or handshake feels confident, comfortable, or warm.

Or does it make you feel so uneasy that you have the desire to withdraw? Are the hands of individuals clammy, indicating nervousness? Or limp, which suggests being timid or noncommittal?

- **Pay Attention to the Laugh and Voice of People**

The volume and tone of our voice can tell us a lot concerning our emotions. Vibrations are produced from sound frequencies. When you are reading a person, observe how the tone of their voice has an impact on you. Ask yourself whether the tone is whiny, snippy, or abrasive. Do they have a soothing tone?

Importance of Nonverbal Communication

Simply put, if you do not know how you are coming across to others, you are losing out on a huge part of human interaction.

If you are a young professional with ambition, discerning these cues could build or mar your career. And if you are in search of how to move up the ladder of your career, being able to take advantage of what you know about body language can give you an upper hand in the presence of your clients, in the office, or in other professional circumstances.

A fast, precise read could make a lot of difference when it comes to messing up in front of your coworkers or dazzling your boss.

Tools and Resources to Help

If you need more resources and tools to help further your knowledge about body language, you should be able to locate some relevant information in the books below.

- Argyle, Michael. *The Psychology of Interpersonal Behavior*. City: Penguin, 1972.

- Axtell, Roger E. *Gestures: The Do's and Taboos of Body Language Around the World*. City: Wiley, 1997.

- Birtwistle, Ray L. *Kinesics and Context – Essays on Body-Motion Communication*. City: Penguin, 1971.

- Bok, Sissela. *Lying: Moral Choice in Public and Private Life*. City: Quartet Books, 1980.

- Carnegie, Dale. *How to Win Friends and Influence People*. City: Simon & Schuster, 2009.

- Caro, Mike. *The Body Language of Poker: Mike Caro's Book of Tells*. City: Carol Pub Group, 1994.

- Cohen, David. *Body Language in Relationships*. City: Sheldon Press, 1992.

- (I975) Bodily Communication, Methuen. Axtell, R.E.

- (I997) Body Language: The Meaning of Modern Sport, Lawrence & Wishart. Bok, S.

- (I999) Body Language: A Visual Guide, Newleaf. Cohen, D.

Courses and Textbooks

- The Nonverbal Communication Reader

- Lie Detection in 100 Minutes

- Nonverbal Communication, 1st Edition

- Nonverbal Communication in Human Interaction

- Manwatching

Body Language Sites:

- [Joe Navarro](#)

- [Statement Analysis](#)

- [Eyes for Lies](#)

- [Science of People](#)

Chapter 3: Body Language Cues - Feet and Legs

Body Language Cues and Meanings Given by Feet and Legs

Legs are exciting in the aspect of nonverbal body language because they offer much insight about us without our knowledge.

When an individual is making efforts to keep his body language in check, they generally focus on the upper body. Thus, the legs might inform us about their thoughts. If your upper body and legs are conflicting, then there is likely calculated control.

The following are some of the cues and meanings given by the legs and feet:

Open Language

- **Standing**

Legs are held separately when standing. They provide a stable foundation for the individual. Standing with feet around shoulder-width apart is a relaxed, standard pose. A bit wider signifies that the person feels confident and grounded.

A broader posture gives the body a fuller look and makes it appear bigger. It is an indication of dominance and power. It takes up more ground.

Taking a firm position is getting the body ready in the event of an attack from the other individual. It can also be a position of vigilance.

Open legs expose and make the genitals vulnerable. It can be a display of power between men or a sexual show, especially from men to women.

When one foot is placed ahead and the other behind, it can be taking a very firm position in the event of a frontal attack. It could equally be a frozen walk that indicates that the individual wants to head somewhere.

- **Sitting**

Sitting with legs open slightly is a position of relaxation. It shows that the person is comfortable. The individual could flop one or both legs down sideways to the extent that they can reach.

Sitting supports a broader opening of the legs and could be a sexual display of the crouch. If the person is bothered about this display, they may use their hands to cover their genitals.

Closed Language

- **Standing**

When an individual is standing with both feet together, it may signify anxiety as it makes them less significant as a mark and offers some security to the genitals.

A completely closed standing situation has knees touching. Enhanced need for security may be signified by the individual turning to the side slightly, leaning a bit forward or pulling back the hips.

Note that this position is closed and also occurs when an individual is cold.

- **Sitting**

When sitting, an individual may hold the knees tightly or gently together depending on their level of anxiety.

- **Crossed Legs**

Similar to the arms, crossed legs can be negative and protective, defending the individual from others and their ideas.

Crossed legs may signify tension and enhanced anxiety, resulting in legs held more flexibly. Crossed legs can also imply that the individual needs to pay a visit to the toilet.

- o Standing

Crossing legs while standing is a sign of being coy or shy. Crossed legs can also be joined with a lowered head or holding hands behind the back.

This position is quite unstable, and the individual may sway a bit. It makes it easy for him to get pushed over, and it is not easy to unwind and run. It is hardly a defensive position, and it could be viewed as a submissive one.

- o Sitting

Crossing legs is less difficult when sitting and can come in numerous forms. When an individual cross his ankles, it is a minimal cross and can be a bit relaxed, especially when he stretches his leg forward and leans back. If he adds more tension to his posture, like in clenching his hand, then it may be an indication of self-restraint.

When a person crosses his ankles and tucks his legs underneath the chair, it can signify hidden anxiety, especially if the individual is leaning forward.

Crossing knees may signify defensiveness or greater anxiety, especially if the legs look tense, and more so if the individual firmly wraps one leg around the other.

An individual holding his knees together may also signify more anxiety than if they fall a bit separate. It could also be a position of female modesty.

A relaxed cross using the lower legs that fall close to one another requires a wider pelvis. Thus, women may use it as a sexual signal, especially if their legs are exposed.

When an individual places one ankle above the knee of the other leg, with the above leg's knee facing sideways, it can be a sneaky crouch display and is done more by men because it calls in females and dares other males. The individual could also cover his genitals with his hands holding the ankle or shin of the top leg.

When the individual holds his crossed legs, it can indicate being self-protective.

Pointing

Individuals can use their legs to point to things that interest them, as with other parts of the body. The reverse is also the case as pulling a leg backward may display disinterest.

- **Standing**

When standing, a person can point a leg at an angle with both knee and foot. For example, during a conversation, an individual who desires to leave points to the door. Pointing in any direction away from the other individual implies that they want to be anywhere but with you.

- **Sitting**

While sitting, legs do not need to support the body, but they have more visibility and tend to send more evident messages except when hidden underneath a table where they may point in the direction of interest subconsciously.

Feet or knees may point toward other interesting individuals. They may also point to the anticipated travel direction.

Sitting forward with a foot pointing back the other away is a readiness to get up and is a popular sign that the individual is planning to head somewhere or leave.

Moving

Moving legs can be a workout to enhance circulation and aid in loosening cramped muscles. They also pass a signal sometimes.

- **Standing**

When an individual is standing and he swings a leg, it can function as a pointer. Bouncing the leg can signify impatience.

Moving a leg is one method of moving closer to another individual without moving the body completely. When it is pulled back, it indicates disinterest. When the leg moves back and forth toward an individual, it may be an elusive game of attraction-rejection that calls on the other individual to chase after you.

If timed correctly with music, especially if the upper body bounces, it could be a dance invitation. Females sometimes do this movement deliberately to make their breasts bounce and draw in a male's attention.

- **Sitting**

Individuals bouncing a crossed leg up and down could be an indication of impatience. It could also indicate attraction, similar to the standing movement. It may equally be a rather evident pointing. When sitting, waving a knee sideways can also signify impatience.

The leg may also be swinging alongside music, which shows that the individual is relaxed and appreciating the vibe.

Walking

Individuals walk in different manners, partly as a result of intent and partly as a result of habit.

A quick walk signifies that an individual is in a hurry or has the characteristic of someone who loves getting things done. An individual who is slower could be one who has a lot of time to spare, is lazy, is daydreaming, or possibly gets pains and aches when walking faster.

A stylish gait shows attention on the self and a specific self-awareness in regard to how others view them. Longer strides signify confidence while shorter steps display preciseness or timidity.

Striking

Legs can equally serve as weapons. Legs have a farther reach than arms and have much larger muscles that ensure a powerful kick.

Touching

- **Standing**

When standing, individuals are not able to touch most of someone else's legs. However, they may be able to stroke the thighs or bottom seductively. One slap may imply, "Let's go!" and signify that the individual is making a suggestion. A slap to the side of the leg may portray irritation.

- **Sitting**

When sitting, a person is able to reach more parts of the leg, especially in the cross-legged position, and in a more evident manner. Thus, stroking seductively can be a powerful sexual invitation.

Preening is also possible by brushing imagined or real bits of dirt off crossed legs. Tapping of legs could be in rhythm to music and could also indicate impatience.

Chapter 4: Body Language Cues - Torso and Arms

Body Language Cues and Meanings Given by the Torso

The shoulders, chest, and belly region make up the torso of our body. The torso is very important in the body makeup and our survival as it is where our vital organs inhabit. Subconsciously, we have an intuitive habit of protecting our torso when threatened or when we feel our personal, private space is being invaded. We also allow access to our torso when we feel relaxed and in a comfortable mood.

Reading a person's body language is greatly enhanced when one understands body posture because the body language portrayed by the torso is subtle. When recognized, however, it can tell a lot about the person with whom one is dealing.

Confidence is always portrayed by a torso that is open, straight, and tall, whereas a person who is defensive, tired, or timid has a torso shaped in a hunched stance.

A conversation between two people is typically going very well when one of the parties involved, through conscious or unconscious actions, mirrors the actions of his fellow conversation partner. This action is called "mirroring" in body language terms. Mirroring is a sign of agreement and comfortability with the conservation by both parties involved. Mirroring starts with body posture.

Body Language Cues and Meanings Given by Arms

The arm is made of a ball up top, a hinge joint in the middle, and a very complex toolset at the end. The arm makes for an interesting appendage in the study of body language signs as it provides a lot of information about the person. The subtle signs given out with the arms are below.

Still arms

Still arms are usually the first telltale sign of a deceiver. A person wanting to deceive tries to keep his intentions in check through the act of maintaining still arms. He usually holds one arm with the other while going through the motions of his deceitful plan.

Arms Expansion

A smart way to appear friendly or as a threat is by the mere usage of the arms as expanding devices. They can help one appear bigger or smaller than one actually is, which is dependent on the situation one is being faced with at the point in time. Arms can offer or show support and comfort when expanded in a curved shape.

When faced with a threatening position, the arms can engage in quick, direct motions toward the threatening source.

The arms also portray the level of a person's confidence or aggressive pose when they are expanded in a lateral manner.

Arms Shaping

Arms shaping is a means of literally telling people the state of one's feelings by the act of waving the arms. The shaping of the arms indicates many things in the study of body language.

In an excited or confident mood, waving the arms in windmill fashion is a telltale sign. In a less confident or depressed mood, the arms aren't waved about wildly but are waved much closer to the body.

A person can be viewed as clumsy when he waves his arms and bangs objects during the act.

Raising Arms

The body language cues shown by raising the arms varies

from exaggeration to frustration to confusion. These gestures are shown when the person throws up his hands.

Frustration is shown when a person throws both arms in the air, a sign that indicates that whatever is troubling the person at that point in time is being thrown up into the air.

Confusion is a state of mind shown by the arms when a person shrugs his shoulders in tandem with the arm-throwing gesture.

Reaching Forward Arm Gesture

An aggressive pose is shown when the arms reach forward in a sudden, direct thrust, especially if the hand is shaped like a fist.

Reaching forward with the arms can also be seen as a supportive or affectionate gesture as portrayed by spouses or lovers when they seek to engage in intimacy with their partner.

Pulling Back of the Arms

The first thing that intuitively comes to anyone's mind when faced with a threatening situation is to pull back the arms because the arms are usually the first body part used to gain an advantage in such a situation when grabbed.

Hidden Arms

Hidden arms, which literally expose the torso, indicate a state of vulnerability in some cases. They may mean one is submissive and can't do anything about the situation with which he is faced. Hidden arms may also mean the person is comfortable with the other party as he believes his open torso isn't vulnerable to attack. Additionally, they may indicate a position of power as the person believes what is before him is not a threat in any way.

Hidden arms may also be indicative of a person's threatening intentions as the arms could possibly be hiding a weapon.

Arms Crossing

When the arms are crossed in front of a person's torso, they act as a barrier or pathway to one's body. Crossing of the arms is used to form a defensive shield when a person feels his personal space is being invaded. Not all crossed arms are signs of defense, however.

- The crossing of the arms could indicate the state of anxiety of a person's mind. It could be that the person doesn't trust the person with whom he is in contact, it could be a feeling of discomfort or pain, and, in some cases, it could portray a sense of déjà vu or vulnerability from an experience of personal trauma.

- The extent to which the arms are crossed is an indication of how closed off a person really is. The gesture can vary from a light arm cross to folded arms to crossed arms wrapped around a person's torso. In extreme cases, the person would have their arms wrapped tightly around their torso with their hands or palms formed into fists, which is an indication of hostility. When the legs are also crossed, it further hints at an extra measure of hostility.

- The crossing of the arms while wrapping them around one's torso could be a sign that the person is trying to rein in his temper or is merely trying to keep his body still.

- Hands in an arm-cross gesture mean the person is in a relaxed, comfortable mood as he is engaged in a self-hug.

- Crossing of the arms is also seen as a compliment in some climes. A person who engages in such arm crossing while listening to the other party is seen to be giving his full attention to the party.

- When the arms aren't crossed, it is indicative that the person is very comfortable with the person or people in his immediate surrounding space. It could also mean that the person feels in a position of power as he feels absolutely no threat from the person he is in contact with at the time.

When a salesperson comes in contact with people who engage in the arms-crossed gesture during their marketing gig, they usually employ the technique of having such people make use of their arms. For example, they could give them a pen to write with to loosen them up and make them more comfortable while they sell whatever product they intend putting in the mind of the person.

Arms as Weapons

Arms as weapons are usually used as a means of defense or attack depending on the situation faced.

Chapter 5: Body Language Cues - Hands and Fingers

Body Language Cues and Meanings Given by Hands and Fingers

The hands come with twenty-seven bones each and are an expressive aspect of our body. They offer us huge capabilities as an advanced species in the way we deal with our surroundings. After the face, the hands are perhaps the best source of body language.

It should be noted that hand gestures vary significantly across cultures and what you deem a normal hand signal in your country could result in you getting arrested in another.

A hand signal could be minor, perhaps trying to betray your subconscious thoughts. It may also be done using both hands while trying to stress a point.

The following are some of the major hand cues in body language:

Holding

- Cupped hands create a container that can hold

something softly. Gripped hands can hold something tightly. Hands can hold together or individually. Cupped hands can signify a fragile idea. They can also be utilized for giving.

- Gripping can display ownership, possessiveness, and desire. The tighter the grip, the more intense the feeling.

- Holding one's self can equally be an act of restraint. It can be to allow the other individual to speak. It can also be utilized when the individual is mad, efficiently preventing them from violence.

- The tension of a holding group shows the amount of pressure the individual feels. Folded arms could be relaxed. However, if the hands are holding the opposite arms, it becomes more preventive.

- Holding hands behind you leaves the front open and can display confidence. Hidden hands may also display tension. When a hand holds the other arm, the tighter the grip and higher the hold determines how great the tension is.

- Both hands can display varying desires. For example, one hand creating a fist and the other holding it back shows restraint from punching someone or something else.

- Also, individuals who are being deceptive often try to keep their hands in check. You may get suspicious when they remain still with one often holding the other. Another signal could be holding them behind. These are only likely signals, and you should also watch out for related signs.

Control

- A hand with the palm facing downward may restrain or hold the other person figuratively. It could be an act of authority like, Stop this instantly! It could also be a request like, Please hold on. This also comes up in the leading hand on top handshake. Palms downward while inclined on a desk usually show dominance.

- An outward-facing palm toward others pushes them away or fends them off in a less subtle method than the palms-down sign.

- A pointing hand or finger informs an individual where to head.

Hiding

- Individuals may hide their hands by placing them in pockets, behind their back, underneath their legs, or underneath the table. Hands are frequently used in communication and the hiding of hands may signal a yearning not to collaborate or communicate. They may be saying, "I don't agree with you" or "I don't want to speak to you."

- Individuals may hide their hands as a deliberate sign of disobedience, like putting their hands in their pockets. Liars may keep their hands hidden out of worry that they may expose themselves.

- Hiding hands may also be a way of listening, passing across the message, "I want to listen, not talk."

- Placing hands behind the back or in pockets can also be due to a feeling of relaxation and not wanting to speak.

Fingers are quite flexible and support subtle signals. Below are a few of these:

Pointer

- A pointing finger signifies direction. For lengthy distances, individuals could point the finger upward in a diagonal manner like shooting an arrow.

- Pointing at others is similar to prodding and is mostly classified as threatening and rude.

- Individuals who are mad tend to point more. This pointing includes at themselves when they feel insulted or hurt and at those they feel are responsible.

Prod

- Prodding can function like a stiletto knife, piercing forward at the other individual. The index finger is typically used, but sometimes the middle finger is utilized. Prodding is usually threatening and taken as a personal attack.

- The prod can also be used in pointing downward at an item that is not there. It is not as menacing as pointing straight at an individual.

Rudeness

- The middle finger pointing up implies a swear and signifies a penis. In this gesture, the little finger suggests that the other individual has a tiny penis. It is sometimes utilized as a rude sign from a lady to a man.

- The initial two fingers pointing upward while the palm faces toward oneself implies f**k off. On the other hand, the palm facing the other individual connotes peace.

Thumbs-up

- Thumbs-up shows agreement and approval. Thumbs-down shows lack of consent. When held sideways, it implies uncertainty.

- Thumbs-up when crossing arms or a single handheld across the chest is a subtle approval sign. It can also be a way of inviting others to show that they approve what you are saying.

- Thumbs that stick out when you place your hands in your pocket are usually an indication of confidence, feeling in control and relaxed. For this reason, the gesture could be a sign of friendliness and authority.

- In a few cultures, giving a thumbs-up implies sexual interest. In other cultures, it might just be rude.

Other Signals

- Crossed fingers show hope.

- Inspection of fingernails portrays disinterest and boredom.

- Fingers fluttering may portray uncertainty.

- Fidgeting fingers may show tension or boredom.

- Sucking of fingers is a relapse to breastfeeding and childhood. It may also portray feelings of inferiority and timidity.

Basic Interpretations of Handshakes and Hand Gestures

Similar to the way a person writes, the way they shake hands offers a clue to their inner nature. So if you are aware of what every handshake says about the people with whom you are interacting, you can make good use of this information.

Below are a few kinds of handshakes and what they mean:

- **Dominance** is displayed with one hand placed above the other, extended holding, and holding the individual using the other hand.

- **Affection** is displayed with the duration and speed of the shake, touching using the other hand, and smiling enthusiastically. Affectionate and dominant handshakes are similar and may result in a confusing situation where a dominant individual act friendly.

- **Submission** is displayed with a floppy hand, palm up (which may be clammy at times), and a fast withdrawal.

Kinds of Handshakes

- **Dead fish:** This form of handshake has no energy, no squeeze, no shake, and no pinch. It makes you feel as if you are holding a dead fish as opposed to a hand. This handshake is associated with low self-esteem.

- **Sweaty palms**: When a person is anxious, their nervous system often gets overactive, which in turn leads to sweaty palms.

- **The two-handed handshake:** This handshake is typically common with politicians. It is a form of handshake that brings to mind words like "friendly," "trustworthy," "warmth," and "honest." If the hand remains on your hand, the handshake is sincere. But if the hand moves to your arms, wrists, or elbows, they wants something from you.

- **Brush off:** This kind of handshake is a fast grasp then a release that seems as if your hand is being pushed aside. The handshake implies that your agenda is not essential.

- **Controller:** If you feel the other person pulling your hand toward him or directing it to another direction or a chair, this kind of person is a controller. It implies that they need to be in control of both animate and inanimate items in the room, including you.

- **Bone Crusher:** This kind of handshake, which has to do with squeezing your hands until you begin cringing, aims to intimidate you. For these individuals, you don't need to pretend to be weak. They might even respond positively if you display your strength.

- **Finger Vice:** When a person grips your fingers as opposed to your whole hand, the aim is to keep you far from them. These individuals are usually secure. If they crush your fingers, they are including a display of personal power aimed to hold you at a distance.

- **The Top-Handed Shake:** As opposed to holding his hand vertically, this shaker does so horizontally so his hand is above yours. This gesture implies he feels he is superior to you.

- **Lobster Claw:** Similar to a lobster claw, the other individual's fingers and thumb touch your palm. This individual is scared of deep connections and may have issues in developing relationships. Give them time and let them open up when they want.

- **The Pusher:** While this individual gives you a handshake, she stretches her arms so you are unable to get close. This kind of individual requires space and is not allowing you in. You must provide them the emotional and physical space they want if you plan on building a friendship with them.

Chapter 6: Body Language Cues - The Face

Body Language Cues and Meanings Given by Facial Expressions

The face consists of about forty muscles. It utilizes many of these in sending numerous nonverbal signals. Alongside muscles, the dampness and color of the skin can also be crucial in communication.

Below are some of the body language meanings and cues given by facial expressions.

Facial Colors

You will be able to tell what a person is feeling by the color of their face. The face generally can switch between colors, all with diverse implications.

Red

- A red face may signify that the individual is hot as the blood heads to the surface of the skin to cool down. The red may also be from either emotional arousal or exercise. It can either be when a person is energized or excited.

- A red face is also typical of individuals who are angry. It is a clear sign of danger, and it is a way of warning the other person that they may be injured if they refuse to back off.

- Other times, individuals blush when they are embarrassed. The necks of some individuals go red, while for others it is the cheeks. Other times, the entire face goes red.

White

- White skin may be an indication of coldness as the blood heads deeper into the body to prevent further cooling.

- White skin may signify fear, usually extreme fear. It also occurs as the blood leaves a surface that has been injured, heading to muscles where its power is required more.

Blue

The skin also can go blue as an indication of extreme fear or cold.

Facial Moisture

- Sweating is the natural cooling mechanism of the body when it gets hot. It can occur as a result of emotional arousal and excitement.

- Sweat is also linked with fear. It is probably to help the skin become slippery to stop an opponent from getting a firm hold.

Facial Expressions

- **Trustworthiness**

According to Helman et al. (2015), it was proven that a face that is trustworthy is one that has a slight smile, with the mouth corners turning upward and the eyebrows a bit raised. This expression implies being friendly and confident without being nervous as to whether others will like us, making us more appealing as friends.

- **Intelligence**

According to Kleisner et al. (2014), it was proven that individuals who have a narrower face with a lengthy nose and thinner chin are a typical stereotype of how a person who is very intelligent looks. On the other hand, a person with a broader, oval face, with a smaller nose and larger chin is seen as having lower intelligence.

They also pointed out that higher intelligence is discerned when a person is showing joy or smiling. On the other hand, lower intelligence is easily linked with untrustworthiness and anger.

Meanings Given by the Eyes and Eye Movement

Here are a few of the facial signals and eye movements you may see for various emotions. Note that these are just possible indicators. Not all signals are required and not all indicated signals here necessarily show the emotion linked to them.

- Anxiety: Damp eyes, eyebrows pushed together, head tilted down slightly, lower lip trembling, and chin wrinkled.

- Fear: Eyes opened wide, pointing down, or closed. Eyebrows raised, white face, head down, open mouth or corners turned down.

- Anger: Wide eyes and staring, pulled down eyebrows, forehead wrinkled, red face, clenched or flattened teeth and flared nostrils.

- Desire: Dilated pupils with eyes wide open. Eyebrows raised slightly, head tilted forward, slightly puckered or parted or smiling lips.

- Sadness: Cast-down eyes that are tearful or damp. Pinched lips, head facing downward or to the side.

- Happiness: Sparkling eyes with crow's-feet wrinkles by the sides, mouth smiling, eyebrows slightly elevated, head level, and possible laughter.

- Envy: Eyes staring, jutting chin, nose crooked in sneer, and corners of the mouth turned down.

- Surprise: Eyes open widely, eyes elevated high, head tilted to the side or held back, mouth dropped open.

- Interest: Fixed eye gaze at an element of interest, could be squinting. Eyebrows a bit raised, lips pressed together slightly, head pushed forward or erect.

- Boredom: Eyes looking in another direction, face generally not moving, head upheld with hand, lips drawn to the side.

- Disgust: Eyes and head turned to another direction, closed mouth, sneering nose, jutting chin, and protruding tongue.

- Relief: Tilted head, mouth either smiling or tilted

down.

- Pity: Eyes probably damp and in extended gaze, head tilted sideways, eyebrows pulled together slightly downward at edges or in the middle.

- Shame: Head and eyes facing downward, blushing red skin, and eyebrows held low.

- Calm: Facial muscles relaxed. Eyes in a steady gaze, mouth possibly turned up a little at the sides in a calm smile.

Chapter 7: Detecting Lies and Deceptions: Do It at Your Own Risk

When spotting lies, individuals often pay close attention to body language or tells. These are behavioral or physical signs that disclose deception. Some of the typical suggestions state that continuous fidgeting, shifty eyes, and evading eye contact are certain signs that the speaker is lying. There are times when body language or subtle cues do not really indicate the signals we understand, however. You may interpret throat clearing as a lie when it is actually just a person clearing their throat.

Although body language cues tend to provide clues to lies, research has suggested that many of the most predictable behaviors do not really relate to lying. According to Psychologist Researcher Howard Ehrlichman, who has been carrying out a study of eye movements for decades, eye movements do not indicate lying at all. As a matter of fact, he proposes that shifty eyes mean that an individual is thinking or just accessing their long-term memory.

Other studies have proven that although individual behaviors and cues are signals of deception, the most common ones associated with lying like eye movements are part of the most unreliable predictors. So although body language can be a tool that is useful in spotting lies, it is essential to know which signals to watch out for.

So, before you decide to assume anything about a deception or lie, be confident you are correct as the cues don't always mean what you think.

How To Spot a Lie/Deception

Research has proven that individuals have the tendency to focus on the appropriate behavioral cues linked with deception. According to a meta-analysis in 2001 by researchers Bond and Hartwig, that while individuals depend on effective cues for lie detection, the issue is how weak these cues are as indicators of deception in the first place.

A few of the most precise cues of deception that individuals focus on consist of:

- Vagueness: If the individual speaking seems to leave out crucial details intentionally, it may be because they are telling lies.

- Vocal ambiguity: If the individual does not seem secure or certain, they may be seen as lying.

- Overthinking: If a person seems to be thinking

excessively hard to fill in the story details, it may be because they are lying to you.

- Indifference: The absence of expression, shrugging, and an uninterested posture can be signs of lies because the individual is making an effort to avoid communication tells and emotions.

The lesson is that although body language can be useful, it is crucial to watch out for the appropriate signs. According to experts, depending too much on signs may hamper the capacity to notice lies. Now, let us look at more active ways of determining if someone is being deceptive.

Request They Tell the Story in Reverse

Detecting lies is often viewed as a passive procedure. Individuals often assume that they will be able to detect the facial expressions and body language of the potential liar to notice obvious tells. However, research has proven that these expressions and gestures are not a great way of detecting lies. Using a more active method to uncovering deception can offer better results.

Enhancing the Mental Load Makes It Harder to Lie

Asking individuals to say their stories the opposite way as opposed to chronological order can enhance the precision of detecting deception. The researchers suggest that nonverbal and verbal cues that differentiate between telling the truth and lies become more obvious as there is an increase in cognitive load.

In essence, it is more mentally taxing to lie than to tell the truth. Also, if you include more cognitive difficulty, behavioral signals can become more obvious. Aside from the fact that it is more cognitively challenging to lie, liars' channel lots of mental energy toward evaluating how others respond and monitoring their behaviors.

They are worried about how credible they are and want to make certain that other individuals find their stories believable. Lying requires a huge amount of effort, so by throwing in a tedious task like reciting their story in the opposite direction makes the story more difficult to tell and it may be easier to spot cues.

Responding to Questions Using Questions

Even liars would rather not lie. Lying outrightly comes with the possibility of detection. Before responding to a question using a lie, a deceptive individual will typically try not to respond to the question at all. One common means of evading questions is to respond using another question.

Signals and Cues to Look for from a Wide Variety of Signs and Cues

There are a few subtle nonverbal cues we tend to miss that indicate that someone is lying.

Clearing of Throat

Clearing of the throat is a form of flight or stress response. The moisture that is usually in the throat redirects to the skin and comes out as sweat.

Hard Swallowing

The absence of moisture in the throat as a result of the flight-or-fight response results in hard swallows. It is also known as Adam's apple jump.

Manipulation of the Jaw

There are liars who open their mouths and begin moving their jaws forward and backward. This jaw movement aids in stimulating the salivary glands behind the throat. They do this movement as a means of moistening their throats, which are dry as a result of the flight-or-fight response.

Pointing Eyes

The eye points to the location the body wants to head. Liars often stare at the closest exit, transmitting their wish to psychologically and physically escape the nervousness their lying causes. People who stare at their watches communicate this message as well. It signals the desire to shorten a conversation.

Pointing Feet

Like the eyes, liars may point their feet in the direction of the door. It shows their desire to psychologically and physically escape a situation that is not comfortable.

Absence of Emphatic Gestures

Liars typically face issues utilizing emphatic gestures like tapping their hands lightly on the table, finger pointing, or forward movement of the head. Denials alongside emphatic gestures are usually a sign of truthfulness.

Backward Movement of the Head

Liars tend to move their heads backward slightly when they lie. This gesture is a subtle way of distancing themselves from the cause of their anxiety. Individuals tend to lean closer to things and individuals they like and move away from things or people they don't like.

Leaning Backward

Liars frequently move their whole bodies backward slightly. Leaning creates a distance between their targets and themselves. The individuals we lie to cause us nervousness because we are scared of being caught.

Subtle nonverbal cues that signal lies or deception can offer extra support to determine if an individual is deceiving you. But do not forget, a single nonverbal cue on its own may not be accurate.

Nonverbal cues are more dependable indicators when they take place in groups. The best method of determining the truth is the comparison of what an individual says to objective facts.

In the absence of these facts, detecting lies will always be a difficult chore. Honest individuals can do and say things that make it seem as if they are dishonest. Also, liars can do and say things that make them seem truthful. In the end, having a lot of evidence is an excellent way of telling the truth from lies.

Chapter 8: How to Quickly Interpret Verbal Communication

The Value of Combining Verbal and Nonverbal Communication Interpretation

Communication has to do with transferring a message. It occurs using words or no words. There are two kinds of communication:

- Verbal

- Nonverbal

So,

- What is verbal communication?

Verbal communication has to do with communicating using words. It is either written or face to face. Technology like the Internet and phone have ensured verbal communication can occur without being in the same location or through writing.

The volume, tone, and sound of spoken words are crucial. Also, connotation (emotions associated with words) and denotation (literal definition of words) are other elements that send the proposed meaning of the message. So, selecting appropriate words according to circumstances is important.

Verbal communication may not be suitable for intercultural circumstances due to a difference in symbols and meanings.

What Is Nonverbal Communication?

Communication that does not involve words falls in the category of nonverbal communication. It is sent as visual cues. Gestures, body language, touch, and facial expressions among others are some examples of this form of communication.

It can be interpreted and noticed better than words as it communicates more messages. It is used for interpreting whether verbal communication is genuine or not.

Nonverbal communication can differ depending on culture and individual differences. There is no precise interpretation; instead, it has open interpretations.

The message intended is transferred to individuals nonverbally by utilizing:

- Body language or kinesics

- Distance and proxemics

- Appearance

- Touching or haptics

- Eye contact

Similarities between Nonverbal and Verbal Communication

Verbal and nonverbal communications are not different in their use. They go hand in hand. Merging of nonverbal and verbal communication makes communication efficient. In many situations, one cannot be present in the absence of the other. For example, screaming in pain and saying something is painful.

According to Edward Wertheim, a researcher, nonverbal communication has a different role to play in communication. It includes:

- Contradiction

- Regulation

- Substitution

- Reinforcement

- Accentuation

You need to learn both forms of communication, and they are not inborn in numerous situations. There are some inborn nonverbal or verbal communications like screaming in pain, laughing, and crying among others. Aside from these, individuals must learn the majority of the nonverbal communications like table manners, etc.

You must utilize these modes of communication together if you want to generate the intended outcome. Using one without the other does not effectively pass a message. Without one, the other is practically useless.

What to Listen for and What It May Mean in Specific Situations

Volume, Speed, and Pitch

Before discussing words, attention must be paid to clues that you can listen for. You will be able to decipher these clues from listening to the sound of the individual's voice.

These clues include volume, speed, and pitch.

One major clue to listen for is volume or how quietly or loudly a person is conversing. In English, the volume can signify numerous things:

- Powerful emotion: If a speaker's opinion on something is very strong, his volume will most likely go up. This volume increase is the case irrespective of if the emotion is negative or positive. Individuals shout when they are mad, but also when they are thrilled.

- Emphasis: If an individual feel that he has something important to say, he will most likely be louder. In between the middle of a monologue, however, a sentence spoken in normal volume stands out loudly.

- Certainty: Individuals who are certain of their views tend to speak more loudly. However, individuals who are not confident tend to speak in a lower tone.

The next clue is speed and how quickly the individual is speaking. Generally, a change from a steady pace of speaking signifies that something crucial is happening. For example:

Slowing down can signify importance because it is a signal that the individual speaking desires that you listen to every word she says.

Speaking faster can signify strong emotions because speakers of English tend to speak faster when they are thrilled about something.

The final cue is pitch or how low or high the voice of the speaker is. In English, increasing pitch toward the end of a sentence typically implies a question. For example, "Did you get the car?"

However, if the pitch of the speaker's voice goes up toward

the end of every one of his sentences, even if they are not questions, it can display uncertainty.

Cues That Tell It All - Context vs. Words

Sometimes individuals say one thing and mean something else. So how do you find out if what a person says is what they mean? There are specific cues you can pay attention to that tell you all you need to know.

For example, your spouse storms into your home one night after work. He is tight-lipped, red-faced, and does not speak to anyone. He throws his suit jacket on the table, sits angrily on the chair, and just stares at the ceiling. You ask, "Are you okay?" and he snaps back in a mad tone, "I am fine!"

Which of the messages do you have a higher probability of believing? His tone and behavior or his words? You are most likely going to believe his tone and behavior.

According to research, when an individual sends an uneven message where verbal and nonverbal messages are different, recipients are more likely to believe the leading nonverbal message as opposed to the verbal one.

In essence, the way individuals say something has more impact than what they say. In a few studies, nonverbal communication has been proven to have around sixty-five percent and ninety-three percent higher impact than the words actually spoken, mostly when the message consists of emotional attitudes and meanings.

Chapter 9: Little-known Ways to Spot Confidence

Comprehensive Self-Confident Body Language Cues and Meanings

First impressions are crucial. Have you ever noticed someone walk into a room who instantly exudes a trustworthy, confident air that just pulls you and others positively? Well, if you have not, there are a lot of people who are capable of this effect. So, how exactly do they do it?

At first, a lot boils down to how you look, from the way you wear your hair to how you dress. However, more important than any other aspect is body language and the way you interact with an individual you are just meeting. But if you do not exercise caution, your body language may be saying something different than what you intend.

People should learn the proper self-confident body language cues, and what they mean, so they don't pass themselves in the wrong light. They include:

Eye Contact

Eye contact is the major tool for creating nonverbal relations with others. It converses your level of interest, involvement, and warmth. When talking to others, it is ideal to look into their eyes directly for no less than two to three seconds before you look away and move on to the next individual. This maintained contact is a sure sign of confidence.

Confident Handshakes

Communication via touch is another crucial behavior. A great handshake is one with complete palm-to-palm contact. A strong handshake along with eye contact and a genuine smile is a great sign of confidence.

Gestures

Gestures include any physical movement that aids in expressing opinions, ideas, and emotions. Punctuating your words using purposeful, lively, spontaneous movement is another primary confidence cue. Do not utilize confusing mannerisms like scratching, playing with hair, ring twisting, and fidgeting, however.

Wardrobe

What an individual wear is another subtle body language cue. Confident individuals dress the part depending on the job or occasion. Business people especially should stay away from busy patterns, showy accessories, revealing necklines, and tight garments.

Authoritative Presence and Posture

Standing up straight and tall sends a message of energy, self-confidence, and authority. What is more, when individuals have great posture, it produces a vibrant attitude of leadership and commanding presence. Bad posture passes a signal that the individual has low energy levels or low self-esteem or self-confidence.

Proper Facial Expression

Each of the seven rudimentary human emotions—contempt, fear, surprise, happiness, disgust, sadness, and anger—have been proven scientifically to have a specific facial expression. Because your facial expressions have a close relation to emotions, individuals cannot control them consciously or voluntarily.

People who are confident have an expression that matches the message they want to pass. Confident people are able to show they are paying attention when they are listening to conversations. They are able to hold a tight smile, occasionally nod, and keep excellent eye contact.

Initiate Interactions

Confident individuals are the ones who first make eye contact. When you notice an individual offering her hand to shake first, after brief eye contact with you, it could be a major body language self-confident cue.

Voice Tone

If you have watched movies or been in a relationship, you may have heard this line: "It is not what you said, it is the way you said it." These individuals were talking about your paralanguage.

If you detach from the actual words utilized, the nonverbal aspects in the voice consist of pacing, pitch, volume inflection, articulation, and voice tone. Similar to facial expressions, individuals should choose the right paralanguage to portray self-confidence because it passes attitude, emotional meaning, and impact.

Attention

When you speak to a person who leans into the conversation and focuses their energy, ears and eyes on you, it is a sign of self-confidence. They clearly convey honor and respect. It also shows they appreciate the chance to meet you.

Small Signs That Show Lack of Confidence

Self-confidence is confidence in your abilities and sustaining a sense of competence.

Self-confidence can help in fueling success, while a lack of self-confidence can hamper it. If you are not sure if you or someone you care about lacks self-confidence, look out for the signs below.

Lack of Eye Contact

Individuals who have no confidence in their abilities and themselves find it hard to meet the gaze of others. If the eye is the window of the soul, an individual who has low confidence may be scared of you seeing right through them and observing their superficial imperfections.

If someone has a difficult time keeping eye contact with you when you are speaking to them, they may possess such a low level of confidence that looking someone in the eyes makes them deeply uncomfortable.

Apologizing for No Apparent Reason

People who lack confidence will apologize even when they have done nothing wrong. They apologize for the behavior of others. They apologize that they did not turn in an assignment early even when they did. They apologize for the quality of an assignment even before receiving a grade.

People who lack confidence try to prevent forthcoming criticism by first criticizing themselves.

They Go Through Their Phones When Alone During Social Events

People who lack self-confidence find themselves unable to stay still while alone in social gatherings. They tend to stare at their phones when they are alone even if they are doing nothing, which can be viewed as a major sign of lacking self-confidence.

They Slouch

Individuals who don't stand tall but instead allow their bodies to slouch downward tend to pass a message that they are not proud of themselves. Taking some minutes every day to pay attention to your body posture can help fix slouching.

Fidgeting

People who continuously tap their foot or twirl their hair or fidget in general portray an absence of confidence.

Sometimes these behaviors come as a symptom of anxiousness. These behaviors can also send the message you are trying to pass across or may disrupt individuals from getting to know you.

Pay attention to the things that trigger your fidgeting and try to swap these habits when these triggers come up.

Defensiveness

When an individual utilizes defensive body language, like crossing the legs and arms, they may be portraying a lack of self-confidence by pushing out others. The motion of closing off portrays discomfort and anxiety in the environment.

Chapter 10: Little-known Ways to Spot Romantic Interest

Comprehensive Attraction/Romantic Body Language Cues and Meanings

When next you are out, pay attention to the things you see. Do you observe any body language that suggests attraction? When people are speaking, do they lean away from each other? Do they lean into each other? Is the lady curling her hair around her finger?

These are a few subtle cues to look out for when spotting romantic interest. These clues are almost unnoticeable, and you really need to concentrate on seeing them. They may not seem important, but once you identify what they are, they will change the game forever.

Below are a few subtle cues that imply attraction:

- Dilated pupils

- The nostrils of men slightly flare

- Men have the tendency to touch their lips or chin

- Women have the tendency to touch their hair or face

Subtle cues that portray disinterest are:

- Men keep their distance when standing

- Men keep their arms closed around themselves

- Women are distracted or fidgety

- Women hold their purses in front of them

Now, let us take a further look at some romantic body language cues and what they mean.

Posture

There are moments when body language, mostly posture, does not properly communicate the signals we understand. We may interpret slouching as a sign of disinterest. We may believe shoulders down relays sadness.

What is crucial about posture when it has to do with attraction, however, is whether your love interest leans away from you or into you. Are their feet facing you or pointed away? Do they look closed or uptight?

Posture is even crucial for your online dating profile pictures. The way we walk, stand, and even head into a room may say a lot of things about us. We may be able to attract interests and attraction with this simple act.

Preening

Preening typically occurs when women fix themselves, usually when they are close to a man with whom they have an interest. Part of it has to do with her wanting to look better for him. It also has to do with her nerve. Another part of it is that there is something amazing about a woman fixing herself up, so watch out for this subtle sign.

Touch

Many men overlook touch when it comes to spotting romantic interest or attraction. Most women do not touch men with whom they have no interest. For a lot of complicated reasons that have to do with evolution, men have the tendency to initiate while women have the tendency to hold back.

While men initiate an obvious touch, women will touch by "accident." If a man brushes against the arm of a woman or gives her a quick pat on the hand or shoulder during a chat, he may be indicating interest.

It is best not to relate every accidental touch as a sign of romantic interest or attraction. What one should be searching for is not a solitary example. One should be looking for a recurrent pattern. If she keeps hitting her elbow against his in a room that is totally empty, she may have a level of attraction for him. If her arm brushes against his in a crowded room, she may be attracted to him, but she may also be lacking space.

Position of Feet

The feet position portrays the path of interest. For example, if a man has an interest in a lady but is too anxious to walk up to her, his feet may remain pointed in her direction. The same is applicable for women. However, women tend to stand with both feet facing inward or pigeon-toed to assume a posture that is more approachable.

Palms Up

When an individual makes gestures with palms facing upward, it is an indication of openness. Revealing the wrists divulges a readiness to be vulnerable, but hands facing downward divulge an attitude that is slightly defensive.

Eye Contact

A brief stare, which lasts for around five seconds, is typically an attraction sign, especially if it takes place recurrently. It might be an offer to approach and begin a conversation. An upward look from a tilted forehead is a gesture that is quite flirtatious.

A long stare or downward look can pass a threatening message.

Natural Smile

A natural smile, creating wrinkles around the eyes, may indicate real interest. When a person smiles just to be polite, the smile only moves muscles close to the lips.

Leaning

Leaning toward a person when seated is an indication of interest. On the other hand, leaning away indicates irritation or disinterest. This move implies that the individual would prefer to be anywhere else.

Mirroring

Copying the posture or gesture of another individual suggests interest. Mirroring does not have to do with copying each movement exactly. For example, if a lady leans forward and smiles, a man who is attracted may lean in as well.

Learning subtle cues changes the game. But you need to

practice continuously. The best method of practicing is to continue observing. Observe individuals and the way they interact. Listen to what their body language says, and if you are able to get close enough, hear what they have to say. Do their words match what their body language says?

You can learn a lot from body language. You can use body language in business, dating, and communication among others. Body language is one of the solutions of connecting with individuals and developing relationships.

Chapter 11: Little-known Ways to Spot Power Plays

What Are Body Language Power Plays?

Body language power plays are nonverbal behaviors carried out by individuals known as power players. They do these plays to claim superiority over another person without speaking a word. Power plays are very common at workplaces, in some homes, and in a host of other locations.

Signs and Situations Where Power Plays Are Used in Nonverbal Communication

There are many situations where power plays are utilized in communicating nonverbally. A few of these are:

- If an individual sets up a meeting with you but insists that you head to their office for no apparent reason. If this individual is your superior at work, this request is quite normal. However, if this individual is in the same rank as you or lower, you need to exercise caution. Request that they head to your office instead or let the meeting take place in a neutral location like the cafeteria or conference room.

- If a person rejects your ideas consistently and insists on new ones in an atmosphere with high pressure.

- If a person looks down on you. Some individuals move their office furniture and themselves to ensure that they always remain at eye level or higher than you. They may be aiming for an advantage in height because they have the feeling you are at an advantage in other areas.

- If a person is determined to use a blank expression to respond to anything you say. A poker face usually implies that he wants to hide his most crucial thoughts.

- If a person touches your arm or hand in a familiar way as if to tell you, "I can handle this; don't stress your little head." You may have larger issues if the individual is touching something else.

When Someone Keeps You Waiting

If an individual purposely keeps you waiting, it either implies that they are not organized or it is a power play. Keeping another person waiting is an effective means of lowering their status and increasing that of the individual making them wait. This power play has the same impact when individuals wait in line at a cinema or restaurant. Everyone believes that the wait will be worth it, or why wait otherwise?

The Head Shrug

When an individual raises his shoulders and pulls his head down between them, he is safeguarding the vulnerable throat and neck from harm. The shrug is utilized when an individual believes something can fall on them. When used in a business or personal context, it indicates a submissive apology, which diminishes your status in any meeting when you are trying to look confident.

When an individual walk past others who are speaking, listening to a speaker, or admiring a view, they pull their heads downward, turn in their shoulders, and try to look less significant and smaller. This move is called the head duck. Subordinates heading toward their superiors may duck, revealing the power play and status between individuals.

Power Plays in the Home

The shape of a dining room table in a home can give you an idea on how power is distributed in that home, presuming the dining room can accommodate a table of any shape and that the table was picked after substantial thought.

Open families prefer round tables while closed families

choose square ones. Authoritative families go with a rectangular table. When you next have a dinner party, try placing the most introverted individual at the head of the table, far away from the door and with their back to it. Simply placing an individual in a powerful seating position urges them to start talking more frequently and with more authority. What is more, others will listen to them.

Seat Arrangement Power Plays

Rectangular Board Tables

On a rectangular table, it is typical that location "A" always commands the most power, something that remains the case even when all individuals at the table have the same status. Also, in a meeting consisting of individuals who have the same status, the individual who sits at location "A" will possess the most influence, presuming his back is not to the door.

If "A" has his back to the door, the individual located at "B" is the person with the most influence and is a powerful contender for "A." Hook and Stridbeck set up some trial jury discussions that showed that the individual who sits at the head location at a table was selected more frequently as the lead, especially if that individual seemed to be from an elevated economic class.

Supposing "A" was in the top power position, "B" would have the next most authority, followed by "D" and "C." Positions "A" and "B" are seen as job-oriented while location "D" is usually taken by an emotional forerunner, frequently a woman, whose interest is in the group's relationship and getting individuals to participate. This data ensures influencing power play at meetings is possible by attaching name badges on the seats showing where you want every individual to sit, offering you a level of control over what goes on in the meeting.

Chair Location

Most power is given to a visitor when their chair is positioned right opposite the competitive location. A typical power play is placing the chair of the visitor as far as imaginable from the desk of the executive into the public or social territory zone, which further minimizes the status of the visitor.

Power Play Handshakes

- **The Power Shake**

At times an individual may want to prove that they have the upper hand, meaning they are powerful and in control. They do it by ensuring that your hand faces down during a handshake. Although your palm does not have to turn over completely so it directly faces downward, the minor turning demonstrates that they are in charge.

Even if a person places his hand in the top position subconsciously, they have an advantage automatically due to the fact that the down position is linked with control and dominance while a palm up expresses passivity and compliance. Even if neither of you are aware of the positions of your hands, the person with their hand on top feels more dominance and the other person feels more docile.

- **The Socket-Wrencher**

This handshake is a common choice for power players and a common reason for watery eyes. The socket-wrencher forcefully grips the outstretched palm of the receiver and simultaneously adds a sharp reverse thrust while making an effort to pull the receiver into his territory.

This move leads to a loss of balance and begins the relationship in a wrong manner. This handshake could mean one of the following:

- The initiator is someone who is insecure and feels only secure in his personal space.

- The initiator comes from a place that has less space

requirements.

- The initiator wants to control you by getting you off balance.

Irrespective of his intentions, he wants the meeting to be on his terms.

- **The Leach**

Some individuals don't know when to stop gripping. They grip your hand, shake it, and hold on until you want to pull off their fingers. This handshake is a subtle method of indicating control. By extending the contact, they are keeping you engaged for a lengthier time than you may have desired.

Chapter 12: Little-known Ways to Bond and Make an Impression with Others

How to Use Body Language to Bond with Others

Every day you pass signals to people. We do this even without noticing it. The way you shake a hand and the way you move your hands, among others, all pass signals. There are things you will be able to do to send signals subconsciously with the help of body language, which will make individuals like you better, or at least offer you the benefit of the doubt.

Below are a few ways you can utilize body language in bonding with others.

Act Like They Are the Most Fascinating Individual in the Room

If you treat the individual you are speaking to like they are the most fascinating person in the room, they will immediately feel great about your communication and probably want to spend time with you.

Do not look at your phone, do not look around the room for individuals you know, maintain great eye contact, and really pay attention to things they have to say.

Body Language and Attitude

Humans have very judgmental minds. In split seconds, the human mind judges if:

- The individual is a threat.

- If the person is attractive.

- If the individual is significant to your social survival.

Listen to this instinct, but only act on it when you have gotten to know the person better. Give everyone the benefit of the doubt, even if you do not know them. Do not judge people until you have at least interacted with them for a bit.

Retain an Open Posture

The way your body is positioned can say a lot about what you are feeling or thinking. If you have a closed body posture, like when you place your head down or fold your arms, people will believe you don't have an interest in starting up a conversation.

However, if your posture is open and your head is up with

your shoulders back, individuals will see you as friendly and welcoming.

Stand Upright

Standing upright can be beneficial to you when bonding with new individuals for a few reasons. First, you will look and feel more confident. It gives you an upper hand when getting into a conversation. Next, you will naturally have a welcoming and open posture. Last, it will let you breathe in a healthier, fuller way, giving your words more power. Your lungs will also get more oxygen throughout the conversation.

Make Eye Contact

There are a host of psychological influences that have a hand in making eye contact between two individuals powerful because the eyes pass numerous nonverbal cues, some of which many people are unaware of passing. It is for this reason that making eye contact with an individual immediately makes you trust that individual, even just a little.

It also proves that you have an interest in the conversation. Make eye contact, and keep it when necessary.

Gesticulate

Gesturing occasionally using your hands and arms can make what you say more compelling to other individuals. If you need to emphasize a specific point, tapping the table can hammer it home. If you need the opinion of someone else, having your hand turned upward makes the request more appealing.

The only issue here is not the kind of gestures you make, but how frequently you use them. Gesturing excessively will make it seem like something is off with you. So have some reservations when using gestures.

Smile

Smiling is recommended, but it should not be immediate. Hold on until you have registered the face of the other person before you smile so it looks like the smile is for them. Everyone likes a smile, and it makes it easier for you to bond with them.

Mimic

Mimicking the individual, you are speaking to can enhance how attractive you are to them. So, when next you are speaking to a person you really like, ensure you focus on their body language and respond using a similar posture or gesture.

How to Give Off Charisma and Openness with Body Language

Charisma is that additional quality that makes you stand out and remain unique in the crowd. It is also that thing that pulls others close to you like a magnet. But this quality is also something we can use to make us appealing to others using our body language.

Charisma in Celebrities

Take celebrities, for example. The majority of them have that quality that makes others defer to them, resulting in us putting them on a pedestal. In reality, to a certain extent, lots of individuals have charisma. The guy at church who everyone loves; the football team captain all girls have a crush on; your doorman who everyone just seems to like.

Most times, these individuals show dominant as opposed to submissive body language and seem to bloom when they have the attention of others. Celebrities love it when people look at them (it is probably why we refer to it as stargazing), but in reality, they gaze a lot themselves. Eye contact is one of the most crucial aspects of the body language of celebrities.

Celebrities make use of what is known as anticipatory scanning when going through a crowd. They pick out and focus on specific individuals irrespective of whether they know they are doing it or not. They smile numerous times and utilize facial expressions that they change continuously. On the other hand, a few recording artists go with the moody, sullen look, which can be as engaging.

Celebrities use a common movement of the head—they toss or tilt the head backward like they are waiting for applause. Open gestures indicate their assurance and confidence of getting the audience's embrace. Their palms are placed upward, and their arms stretch out like they are drawing the audience toward them. There are a few gestures that are purposely seductive like hair stroking, touching individuals in the front row, etc. These are just a few ways celebrities give off charisma.

Now, let us take a look at how you can ooze charisma yourself.

Offer a Firm Handshake

Your handshake passes a lot of information to others about you. If it is too loose, you seem to lack confidence or appear incompetent. If it is too firm or hard, you may seem uptight or aggressive, making it hard for others to work with you.

An ideal handshake is one where you don't shake the hand of

the person but instead hold the hand gently while applying pressure. It is a great idea to hold on until the other individual let's go because letting go too fast can send the message that you are in a hurry.

Weak handshakes also indicate a lack of confidence and authority. Adapt your handshake to every person and circumstance, making certain it remains firm without seeming aggressive.

Monitor Your Blinking

This suggestion may not be an easy one because blinking is involuntary and trying to control it may not seem natural. But blinking excessively can make it seem as if you are uncomfortable with your interaction with the other individuals.

If you find out you are blinking excessively, try to close your eyes for a few seconds to see if it slows down.

Lean In

By leaning in, people will feel like you are listening to them, which is very crucial. When you want to respond to the individual, you may slightly lean back, offering the other person an opportunity to lean in.

Leave Your Body Open

Another crucial aspect of charismatic body language is leaving your body open. Basically, this suggestion implies that you don't want to place objects between you and other individuals. For example, don't cross your arms or your legs. Also, don't stand facing the bar or hold your drink in front of you. These postures may be considered defensive.

Chapter 13: What Everybody Ought to Know about the Four Basic Personality Types

Overview of the Four Personalities Using the Model from "Personality Plus"

The Four Personality Types

Personality Plus speaks about four core types of personalities. Any system like it must generalize a bit to try to find a middle ground between accurate portrayals and a suitable amount of types. The Personality Plus model permits extensions by merging profiles, like describing an individual as choleric-sanguine as opposed to just sanguine or choleric.

This system exists not to just describe the personality type of an individual, which is the case with the Myers-Briggs system, but to point out those areas of personality that relate to communications between individuals.

The four personality types include:

Sanguine

This kind of personality is linked with air, and they are described as optimistic, spontaneous, and enthusiastic. These kinds of personalities are often characterized with love of going on adventures and coming across new occurrences in life. Aside from being energetic and curious, their way of identification is impulsiveness, which is how they make their decisions the majority of the time.

These individuals are extroverts. They tend to have more fun when around groups of individuals. What is more, they are quite enigmatic and emotional and can start a conversation quickly with anybody. For this reason, it is ideal that individuals with this form of personality to be mindful of keeping their emotions under control as it could result in regrets. Individuals with this form of personality are seen as entertainers because they enjoy attention and activities that are meant to attract attention.

Choleric

The choleric temperament is linked with fire. Individuals who have this temperament tend to be extroverted and egocentric. They may be restless, impulsive, and excitable, and they have reserves of passion, aggression, and energy that they try to encourage in others.

They tend to be task-oriented and are fixated on efficiently completing a job. They can be strong-willed and ambitious, and they love being in control. They can display leadership, are great at making plans, and are often solution-oriented and practical. They appreciate getting esteem and respect for their work.

Tutorially, the ideal means of reaching out to them is via mutual respect and proper challenges that identify their abilities.

Melancholic

The melancholic temperament is linked with the earth element. People having this temperament may seem introverted, suspicious, cautious, and serious. It is possible for them to become engrossed with the cruelty and tragedy in the world, and they are prone to moodiness and depression.

They may be meticulous and focused. These individuals love doing things on their own, both to meet their standards and because they are not naturally sociable.

Educationally, the best method is to waken their compassion for others.

Phlegmatic

The phlegmatic temperament is linked with water. Individuals having this temperament may be private, inward, patient, tolerant, thoughtful, and calm. They tend to possess an abundant inner life, they look for a peaceful, quiet atmosphere, and they are satisfied with themselves. They tend to be consistent and steady with their conduct and thus have faithful and steady friends.

Educationally, you can awaken their interest by experiencing the interest of others in a subject. Individuals having this temperament may seem clumsy or ponderous. Their speech tends to be slow or seem hesitant.

Main Questions to Ask to Determine Your Personality

Are You an Introvert or an Extrovert?

Introversion and extraversion are directions to life. What charges you and where do you love to direct your attention?

Some individuals would rather play inward and pay lots of attention to their inside world of ideas and thoughts. These introverts have more reservation and require time by themselves to recharge. Introverts typically pause and think before taking action or speaking.

Individuals who are introverts are often thought of as shy. However, not every introvert is shy. Some just enjoy spending time alone. In relationships, many introverts will pick a few close friendships over a considerable amount of connections.

Other individuals would rather turn externally to the outer world of things and people. Extroverts are more expressive and outgoing. They feel invigorated by being active and social. Many extroverts love thinking aloud. They talk before they think and love having lots of individuals in their lives.

Are You People-Oriented or Goal-Oriented?

Individuals who are people-oriented build communities and relationships. When executing a task, they love focusing on the human area of things. For example, they are interested in how a task can be least difficult on the individuals who are a part of it.

These kinds of individuals tend to:

- Focus on the requirements of individuals around them.

- Want to develop relationships and keep people happy.

- Place more significance on the happiness and feeling

of people than the task at hand.

Goal-Oriented Individuals

These individuals have a stern mindset about the goals they need to accomplish or achieve. They do anything to achieve the goals they have set. They are disposed to taking risks to fulfill their dreams. It is possible for anybody to set goals, but it needs dedication, work, courage, and confidence to see them through.

Goal-oriented personalities tend to:

- Focus on their goals and the things they hope to accomplish.

- Be concerned with productivity and efficiency.

- Have concrete goals and detailed lists.

How Most People Are a Combination of at Least Two of Them

Every individual has a few or all these affinities at various times and in certain circumstances. But most individuals usually have one or more of these traits that seem to suit them properly in their daily behavior. Additionally, one or two of these traits may not suit them properly, and these traits may even seem alien to their attitude toward life.

A balance of all four traits shapes how every individual view life and those surrounding them.

Basically, an ideal temperament should be a balance of people-oriented and goal-oriented personalities.

When a person is people-oriented, they have the tendency to be motivated to create great working relationships with supervisors, subordinates, and coworkers. These people often possess great communication skills and are bothered about the well-being of their work. They also care about the physical environment and have the tendency to teach, share information, and train.

On the other hand, the goal-oriented personality places all their efforts in accomplishments. These kinds of individuals have an interest in following rules and developing systems and structures to enhance productivity. They are also likely to work best when they focus on measurable, tangible objectives.

It is not necessarily correct to believe that an individual who is goal-oriented cannot be people-oriented. Understanding whether or not your supervisors, coworkers, and others are driven by tangible structures and goals or human relationships can aid you in understanding how to work properly with various individuals.

Importance of Recognizing People by Their Personality

It is crucial to recognize individuals by their personality because it aids in making communication easier in numerous ways:

It Lets You Understand Them Better

By recognizing individuals based on their personality type, you may be able to better understand all the various perceptions and reactions that other individuals have to similar situations. We all have distinct ways of interacting and viewing the world. No kind of personality is better than any other; it is only distinct. Also, every perspective offers something interesting and new.

People often make the mistake of believing that many others share the same opinions, traits, attitudes, and views as they. Highlighting your personal preferences and having the capacity to have a look at a few of the characteristics other individuals have can be insightful for lots of people.

Understanding a few of your key personality traits alongside those you are close to can also be beneficial in relationships. For example, if you are an extrovert and your partner is an introvert, you will have a less difficult time spotting the signs of your partner getting tired. You will also be able to tell when they require time off from socializing. By better understanding the personality traits of one another, you will be able to better respond to the requirements of those you love and develop more powerful partnerships.

It Can Aid You in Identifying What Others Like and Dislike

Perhaps you observed that someone always hated speaking with others, but you never actually knew why. Or maybe you observed your partner requiring additional time to gather their thoughts about an issue before making a decision.

By learning more about where others lie in the aspect of introversion and extroversion, you may be able to understand better why they prefer specific things and do not like others. This understanding may be useful when you want to make crucial decisions that affect your life, like choosing a job in another city.

Learning more about the personality types of others can also aid you in discovering new methods of dealing with issues. If you find out that someone has the tendency to have a high level of introversion, you will know in the long run to give them lots of time to get comfortable in a situation.

For example, knowing what may work best for the personality

type of your employee can give you an idea on how they cope with issues, deal with stress, and manage their work habits.

You Will Have a Better Understanding of Their Weaknesses and Strengths

Understanding the people with whom you work can be crucial in a broad range of situations. You may recognize that the specific aspects in the personality of someone you work closely with serves as a strength in some areas and a weakness in others.

For some individuals, their detail-oriented personality and organizational capabilities can be very useful at work. However, it can also be an issue in circumstances when you have to allow other individuals to take charge.

Note that understanding your personality type and that of others does not provide you with all the answers. Personality quizzes and tests can be helpful, fun, and informative, but even the most elaborate assessments cannot be precise in evaluating what a person can accomplish or who they may be later in life.

Chapter 14: If Someone Is Extroverted and Task-Focused

The Choleric Personality

An individual who has a choleric personality is classified as a person who has dominance in testosterone. That said, a majority of the individuals with this temperament are men, and if there were women, it would be a rare occurrence. An individual with a choleric temperament is impatient, strong-willed, extroverted, and active.

But the choleric person is equally confident, independent, decisive, and practical. Also seen as a visionary, this individual always has lots of ideas. He is goal-oriented and equally a planner. These individuals are associated with the fire element and can be egotistic. This individual is an aggressive type and always wants to be in control.

Basic Qualities of the Choleric Personality

Below are a few qualities of the choleric temperament.

They Are Extroverted

Choleric personalities are extroverted because they will interfere in the affairs of others and say what is on their mind if needed as opposed to minding their business. They respond properly to new occurrences and search for thrills. They speak their mind often but are not always wary of their speech.

They Are Dominant

Their drive for dominance and pride, as well as the way they openly express their emotions, naturally results in outright aggression when you challenge them. They will get angry and want to prove that they are the strongest and biggest and show their superiority. These individuals are pragmatic and do what is required bluntly as opposed to bothering about fantastical situations.

They Are Individuals of Enthusiasm

These individuals are not satisfied with the norm, and they desire immense success in all affairs of life ranging from huge businesses, huge fortunes, a predominant position, and a distinguished reputation.

Ambition is the natural virtue of the choleric individual. His zeal to succeed and excel loathes the vulgar and minimal, and he aims to be heroic and noble.

In his desire for amazing things, the choleric person is aided by:

- A strong intellect. The choleric individual may be gifted with immense intelligence.

- A strong will. The choleric individual is not scared by challenges. But in the event of issues, he displays his energy and endures under immense difficulties until he has attained his objectives.

- Powerful passions. The choleric individual is passionate. Whenever he aims to fulfill his objectives or comes across opposition, he is overtaken with passionate thrill.

- The choleric individual's subconscious instinct is to dominate other individuals. The choleric is born to rule. He feels happiness when he is holding a commanding position to organize huge groups and pull others to him.

How to Spot a Choleric Personality

It is effortless to spot an individual with a choleric personality based on the way they act and speak.

- These individuals aim to be directors and leaders. They always look for ways to be in charge of situations, to be the best, and to be on top. This fact does not mean they have the drive to get to the top of the corporate ladder on a global level or that they desire to have leadership positions, but instead they have the tendency to prevail in daily interactions with other individuals.

- The choleric individual uses commanding, imperative language. They say things as orders as opposed to requests. They are forceful and firm in the way they approach issues. They rely on tough love and make efforts to assist other individuals by pushing them to prove themselves just like they would in the same position.

- The majority of bullies have choleric personalities, but few choleric individuals are bullies. Many would help stand against those bullying others as opposed to allowing them to get away with things. Their demanding and confident nature results in them being natural leaders.

- These individuals would aggressively challenge orders to show their respect for the strength of people. They believe it is crucial for one to prove oneself. They are pushed by a need to prove themselves better than any individual with whom they are arguing to prove that they are correct as opposed to reaching some form of compromise or truth.

- The choleric can lie to keep a position that is dominant. They enjoy competition but don't like losing.

- These individuals defy authority and challenge leaders as if to push them off the leading position and proclaim their dominance as the leader of the pack.

- These individuals can be quite condescending to individuals they look down on. They also take pleasure in the humiliation, misfortune, and pain of individuals with whom they are not on great terms because it is pleasurable for them to have a feeling of superiority over others.

Chapter 15: If Someone Is Introverted and Task- Oriented

The Melancholic Personality

The melancholic personality is a kind of individual who is considered an introvert. This individual is private, logical, and analytical. This kind of individual is careful and takes time when responding to others because they can be suspicious and skeptical.

This kind of person does not have as much confidence as a person with a choleric personality. The melancholic individual bothers about the way people feel about their work.

Being a perfectionist is a trait associated with this individual. Individuals with this kind of personality, due to compassion for others, can be moved to tears. Staying organized is also normal for these kinds of individuals, and when they seem to have a mess around them, they are aware of where to locate what they require.

A melancholic individual wants reassurance and feedback. They also desire the reason behind everything. This individual also asks questions repeatedly because they are scared of making the wrong choice. In essence, this person is no risk-taker and does not want to be seen as inept.

Basic Qualities of the Melancholic Personality

The melancholic personality possesses many qualities.

Disposed to Reflection

When the melancholic individual thinks, they can turn to reflection with ease. They have far-reaching thoughts. The melancholic individual dwells in the past and preoccupies himself with events from way back. This individual is not pleased with the superficial, is penetrating, looks for the reason things occur and how they corelate. He also searches for the rules that have an impact on human life and the values to which man must act.

The thoughts of the melancholic person are broad, and he looks into the future at all times.

Loves Withdrawal

The melancholic person does not feel comfortable when in a crowd for any period of time. He loves solitude and silence. This personality loves to keep away from the crowd and tends to forget his surroundings. He makes tends to use less of the physical senses like his sight and hearing. He is often distracted by company because he is engrossed in his own thoughts.

Serious Notion of Life

The melancholic individual always views life from a very serious perspective. There is a sadness at the core of his heart.

Passive Temperament

This personality type has a passive temperament. It is not easy to push him into fast action because he has a marked inclination for inactivity and passivity. This passive approach to life accounts for his suffering and fear. It also accounts for his fear of self-denial.

They Are Reserved

He finds it hard to create a new connection and does not speak much in the midst of strangers. He reluctantly lets out his inner thoughts only to individuals whom he trusts. This personality does not find the appropriate words to describe and express his sentiments.

He frequently makes efforts to express himself because it

provides him with actual relief when he passes the depressing and sad thoughts burdening his heart to an individual who identifies with him. However, this individual should be a person he categorizes as a friend.

They Are Not Decisive

Due to numerous considerations and fear of hardships and the likelihood that his works or plans may not work out, the melancholic individual has difficulty making a decision. He is motivated to postpone his decision. He puts off things he could do now to later. He may forget about it altogether, and things he should have achieved in an hour end up taking weeks and even months.

They Are Proud

He does not look for recognition or honor and is very much scared of humiliation and disgrace. The melancholic person often shows immense reservation and thereby offers the impression of humility and modesty. In reality, he only withdraws because he is scared of being shamed. He lets others gain preference over him, even if they have less qualifications for a specific position, but he also feels cheated because no one appreciates his talents .

Perfectionism

The melancholic person is frequently a perfectionist. They are quite particular about their desires and in some cases, how they want to achieve them. This perfectionism can lead to them not being satisfied with their own creative works or performance. What is more, they always point out to themselves the areas that should and could be improved upon.

The melancholic individual holds others and himself to high standards that are not realistic and gets distraught when he or others are unable to meet his set standards.

How to Spot a Melancholic Personality

This kind of temperament is sometimes seen as unattractive. According to studies, individuals with this form of temperament tend to suffer from depression and other mood disorders. This personality type is introverted, and they are sometimes viewed as impossible loners. But there are many amazing traits and benefits of this temperament as well.

Below are a few ways you can spot an individual with a melancholic personality.

They Have a Likelihood to Argue

The melancholic individual has a tendency to argue because they cannot let things go if they don't seem right. He offers legitimate, comprehensive arguments utilizing logic, reason, explanations, and evidence analytically delivered or with pleading. He argues only to set things that are wrong right as opposed to asserting dominance.

They Are Possessive

An individual with this personality is possessive about their belongings and is unwilling to lend them to others or allow others to utilize them because they give their own items proper treatment and have a deep care for everything and will be concerned that others will not show the same level of care.

They Are Sensitive

Melancholic people are quite emotional. They are deeply moved by distress and beauty. Due to their tendency for perfection, they can be hurt easily. Their moods are similar to fragile glass sculptures, which are slowly built up, carefully and deliberately, but easy to break and difficult to fix once broken.

They respond to things they don't like with tears and misery as opposed to anger. They do not snap quickly but will hang on to emotions for a lengthy period. These individuals tend to hold a grudge because people who were unable to meet their set standards or have hurt them will not meet those standards without a drastic change.

They Are Pessimistic

This individual is shy and nervous when called upon to start a new job, to go on a new journey, or to carry out a difficult task. They have no courage but do have a strong will combined with power and talent.

It has, therefore, become proverbial that if you throw a melancholic individual in the water, he will teach himself to swim.

If a melancholic person faces hardships in his undertakings, irrespective of how minimal, he loses his spirit and has the urge to give up as opposed to dealing with the issue.

They Are Slow

The melancholic individual takes his time to think. He believes it is crucial to put everything into consideration numerous times before he can establish a safe and calm decision. He is slow in speaking, and if you call him to speak or quickly respond without adequate preparation, or he is worried that a lot is dependent on his response, he becomes fidgety and doesn't find the appropriate words, thus resulting in him providing unsatisfactory and false replies.

The slow speed in thinking may be a reason the melancholic person stutters often, does not complete statements, looks for the proper expression, or utilizes inappropriate phrases. He is not lazy but is slow at his job. He works reliably and carefully, but only if he has adequate time and is not rushed. Naturally, the melancholic individual does not think of himself as a slow worker.

They Are Self-Motivated

The perfectionism of melancholic people makes them extremely self-motivated. Their standards motivate them more than the threat of punishment or reward. They would prefer if they are given multiple opportunities to do something because they believe they can do better the second time. This drive to attain perfectionism and be the best is all the motivation they will ever require.

Melancholic People Are Loyal

The temperament of the melancholic individual pushes toward intense loyalty of family, employees, and friends.

These individuals must earn their loyalty but the instant it is earned, it is for life. The melancholic person is quick to make commitments and promises to individuals with whom they are loyal. Also, they will exceed or meet these commitments for those people for whom they care deeply.

Chapter 16: If Someone Is Extroverted and People-Oriented

The Sanguine Personality

People who are sanguine are easily aroused. Also, what influences them makes them vehemently excited. Their reactions are almost instantaneous. However, an impression is short lived. When the impression is remembered, it really does not lead to fresh excitement.

Basic Qualities of the Sanguine Personality

Superficiality

Sanguine individuals do not have a reputation for discovering the essence of something or having an in-depth knowledge of anything. They appear quite content with surface knowledge. Prior to becoming an expert in any field, the sanguine person is most likely to lose interest because of the presence of a fresh impression to which he is attracted.

He is in love with anything that gets his attention. He really does not like anything that involves deep thought or an enormous amount of effort. It is undoubtedly challenging to make a sanguine person recognize that they are superficial. In the mind of the sanguine individual, they have a clear and perfect understanding of the matter at hand.

Instability

The impressions that get the attention of a sanguine person are very short lived. As a result, there are usually a series of impressions resulting in a considerable degree of instability. This attribute of sanguine people has to be considered by those who have any form of dealings with them, thus helping such people avoid disappointment.

Tendency to the External

Sanguine individuals are not comfortable directing their attention inward. Rather, they prefer looking outward. The sanguine person is the exact opposite of a melancholic one who has a reputation for being introspective. The melancholic person prefers giving all their attention to thoughts that are deep. It really does appear like they do not give any attention to external elements. One major way in which the sanguine person's interest is in the external is the level of attention they put into their appearance as well as the appearance of people around them. They pay attention to attractive faces, good manners, and nice attire. The sanguine individual makes active use of their five senses. On the other hand, the choleric person makes use of will and reason, while the melancholic individual is more reliant on their feelings. The sanguine person hears all that there is to be heard.

They also see it all and say it all. Sanguine people are popular for being lively in speech. Their flow of words and the apparent inability to run out of topics of discussion make the sanguine individual stand out.

Optimism

It is normal for sanguine people to see the world from an optimistic perspective. They have a reputation for overlooking difficulties and are always certain that things will turn out as planned. When things do not turn out as planned, they do not worry themselves for too long—they simply console themselves and go on like nothing happened. The sanguine person has a cheerful attitude, which explains their reputation for always teasing those around them. They do not really give it a thought when people accept their teasing and jokes in a good way. However, they are usually taken aback when people get offended by their jokes and tricks.

Absence of Deep Passions

Sanguine people have passions that are easy to activate.

Nonetheless, their impressions are very short lived.

Practicality

The sanguine person is endowed with common sense. They are known to be practical and rational.

Ways to Tell Someone Is Sanguine

The sanguine person is endowed with many qualities that colleagues and friends consider valuable.

The Sanguine Person Is Extroverted

It is easy for them to get along with other people. They are talkative, easily become acquainted with strangers, and communicate well.

They have a friendly behavior and speech pattern, which makes it easy for them to entertain the individuals around them with stories.

The sanguine individual has a pleasant personality. Additionally, they are always ready to be of assistance to people, although their kind of assistance is not as warm as the melancholic individual's or distant and cold as the choleric person's. Nonetheless, sanguine people will be of assistance in the ways that they can.

They Have a Compassionate Attitude

They appear to have the ability to make their colleagues and friends see their errors in a way that is regarded as generally nice. Correcting others is not something that they struggle to do. If bad news must be broken to an individual, then someone with a sanguine personality should be given the responsibility to do so.

When offended, it is easy and predictable for a sanguine person to react violently. Nevertheless, they can be appeased easily and will not have any bad feelings after a short while. Forgiving and forgetting is not a challenge for the sanguine population. As a result, they expect other people to follow suit.

The Sanguine Individual Is Effortlessly Obedient, Compliant, and Flexible

An individual that is sanguine has many qualities that management considers valuable.

They are quite open and will not find it difficult to talk to people about their challenges and difficulties.

When they are shown their flaws, sanguine people do not get

offended. They accept corrections in the right manner.

Sanguine individuals are known for being excellent motivators. They serve as a form of encouragement to those around them. Additionally, they see things from a positive perspective and would go to any length to make people see things from their point of view.

Self-Importance and Pomposity

Pride in the sanguine person is not like pride in the choleric or melancholic personalities. In the sanguine population, pride is usually manifested as an overvalue of one's worth.

Inclination to Jealousy and Flirtation

Love for the sanguine person is not deep or lasting. Nonetheless, the sanguine person can get jealous, as well as flirt very easily.

Cheerfulness and Love of Pleasure

Sanguine people are not comfortable being alone. They love to be entertained as much as they love being around others.

Weak Abilities to Perform Hard Efforts

Sanguine people do not excel at tasks that require them to give up some form of pleasure. Some of these things involve giving up food, entertainment, and company.

Chapter 17: If Someone Is Introverted and People-Oriented

The Phlegmatic Personality

The observer considers the phlegmatic person to be stubborn and very slow paced. While going through life, phlegmatic individuals are known to carry out their activities very quietly; they try to do just a little and are known to use up only a little amount of energy. It remains unclear whether phlegmatic people do not like using up their energy or if they do not have much energy. Phlegmatic people have a reputation for being task-oriented. They also have the right capacity to carry out activities that need a lot of accuracies and precision and do not need a lot of energy to be expended. The only way a phlegmatic individual regenerate is by sleeping.

Basic Qualities of the Phlegmatic Personality

They Are Glad to Have the Ability to Stick to Rules

The phlegmatic personality type does not delight in breaking rules. They have a huge feeling of discomfort when they think they have performed below expectation or gone contrary to a rule. They sometimes even feel guilty. If there is any form of uncertainty about the best line of action, you can be certain that phlegmatic people will like to know that the best decision is being made. Regardless of the fact that every other person is breaking a rule, a phlegmatic individual will not do so. They would rather stay out.

They Are Interested in the Happiness of Others

Sometimes the fact that phlegmatic people want others to be happy is seen as an absence of confidence. Phlegmatic individuals put other people ahead of themselves. They view it as a move to coexist peacefully with others. It also shows the love they have for those around them. They have a form of confidence in their manner of approach because they know exactly what to do to ensure that conflict is resolved completely. They make every choice with a desire to ensure that there is a form of "niceness" in every circumstance. They do this irrespective of what they might have to give up on.

Their Emotional IQ Is High

Phlegmatic people have a type of personality that is stuck in their own feelings as well as the feelings of the world. When they are meeting people for the first time, because of their personality type, phlegmatic individuals can successfully tell how a stranger feel. That is not all. They can bring up a solution to a circumstance that has the great potential of being bothersome. They do not like seeing other people's feelings hurt. They also do not like to be hurt emotionally. Because they are interested in just positive vibes, phlegmatic individuals have almost made it a norm to carry the burdens of those around them.

They Have Formed the Habit of Always Blaming Themselves

Blaming themselves for things shows that they have a high emotional IQ. As far as they will go to make people feel more at peace, they will go on to blame themselves to ensure that a situation gets resolved. They will even take the blame for the mistakes of other people. They may say a negative occurrence happened because of their carelessness when in reality, it didn't. They make this statement to ensure that everyone around them is relaxed and at peace. They are not selfish in their ways. They usually think about the effects the situation will have on many people instead of its effect on just one person.

They Can Be Trusted

It is the belief of most phlegmatic people that their word is their bond. They will most likely keep a promise that they have made. If they are not able to do so, they will be going against rules and will not be happy about it because they regard expectations from society, as well as traditions as checks in very much the same way as firms have policies.

They Will Defer Decisions to Others when Possible

Deferring decisions is about creating peace in the world. Phlegmatic people will allow another person to decide if there are chances that people will become offended by a decision that they have made. This deferment is one of the ways they try to take care of everyone's emotional needs. As a result of this attitude, a lot of people are of the idea phlegmatic individuals are followers when in the real sense they are big-time leaders because they can give up decision making to other people and give more attention to their strengths, one of which is helping other people develop emotionally.

They Prefer Having Their Time for Themselves

This personality type is one that is characterized with watching movies and relaxing, and they are absolutely comfortable doing so on their own. They are okay being close to just a group of friends. They prefer living in ways that do not require them to have to constantly deal with surprises. Relaxing in a chair with a pet is enough fun for this personality type.

Phlegmatic people seem very much interested in the creation of moments of Zen in a world characterized by stress. They might appear to be quite reluctant. Still, they will go to any length to make sure that rules are adhered to in order to ensure that everyone has a fair chance at being successful even if they, themselves, are affected.

How to Tell Someone Is Phlegmatic

Phlegmatic people do not have an attitude that suggests that they are more important than others. They are not known to assert themselves, and they are known for giving in to other people's wishes in an effort to please others.

They choose to do tasks that offer the smallest amount of resistance. They are very needy of peace. They try to avoid brawls irrespective of what it will cost them, and they want everyone to be friendly with each other.

They Are Terrified by Conflict

They do not have a reputation for starting or provoking conflict (although this fact may not always be true in situations considered to be extreme). Also, they try to stop conflict when it arises. If they get caught up in an argument, they are distressed and upset. They prefer to escape instead of emerging victorious.

- They easily admit a wrongdoing so that aggression is prevented.

- They believe a lot of people know more than they do.

- They always want peace and are not very interested in winning.

- They behave in a very respectable manner. You almost never find them going against rules.

- They never want to cause others any trouble. As a result, they put others ahead of themselves.

They Are Indecisive

They function excellently when given instructions to follow. Also, they follow naturally.

When expressing themselves, they rely on uncertain words and phrases including "perhaps" or "something."

Instead of doing something wrong, they prefer to do nothing.

They can easily alter their paths because of others. When they come across obstacles while on a certain path, they prefer to go around the obstacle instead of going through it.

They Are Calm

Phlegmatic people enjoy being alone. They are introverts. Regardless, they are a lot more sociable than melancholic people because they are not judgmental.

They enjoy hanging out with friends. They are loyal and can stick by a friend regardless of what their friend is facing because they put other people ahead of themselves. They might remain friendly with people even if they want to leave because the other person is unwilling to let go.

They almost never get angry and only get angry after they have been taken advantage of for extended periods. When they get angry, they prefer withdrawing instead of hurting other people.

They are quite confident when they are in familiar situations. However, when they find themselves in situations that they do not understand, they get jittery. They like living lives that are steady and calm and devoid of unnecessary surprises.

They do not want to disturb people with what they have on their minds. They are also scared of being judged. As a result, they do not really tell people what is on their minds.

They listen excellently and attentively to what others have to say without judging or providing any advice if advice is not needed.

Conclusion

Body language is as crucial as writing, listening, speaking, and reading in communication. As a matter of fact, it could be argued that it is more critical because less than ten percent of what we utilize in communication with others takes the form of words. It was only recently that attention moved to the nonverbal aspects of communication.

We utilize body language to send unspoken thoughts, and we tend to believe that no one will understand what we mean. A lot of body language takes place subconsciously, and you may not even know that your hand movements, sighs, facial expressions, and so on are passing messages of interest, affirmation, or dislike.

It is crucial to learn how to read people and the hidden messages they are trying to send. Thus, you are able to tell how a person feels or what they want even without them saying anything.

I hope that this book has provided you with the information you require to become a better communicator. By following what this book teaches, you will be able to enhance your performance and self-confidence. You will also begin to observe the benefits at work, in your relationships, and in your daily encounters with other individuals.

Made in the USA
Monee, IL
03 July 2020